MOUNTAIN STORM, PINE BREEZE

MOUNTAIN STORM, PINE BREEZE
Folk Song in Japan

Patia R. Isaku

THE UNIVERSITY OF ARIZONA PRESS
Tucson, Arizona

About the author...

PATIA ISAKU, ethnomusicologist and student of the Far East, studied folk song in Japan on a Fulbright Grant, eventually becoming a performer and singing in the Sōma Festival for Souls in 1969. An American who studied composition at Oberlin, Ms. Isaku did graduate work in Asian studies at the University of Michigan, and has pursued her research in Japanese music with Madame Abiru Hiroka, Koizumi Fumio, and others at Wesleyan University.

THE UNIVERSITY OF ARIZONA PRESS

This book was set in 11/12 pt. V.I.P. Times Roman

Copyright © 1981
The Arizona Board of Regents
All Rights Reserved
Manufactured in the U.S.A.

Library of Congress Cataloging in Publication Data

Isaku, Patia R.
   Mountain storm, pine breeze.

   Bibliography: p.
   Includes index.
   1. Folk-songs, Japanese—History and criticism.
2. Folk music—Japan—History and criticism.
I. Title.
ML3750.I8   784.4′952   81-706

ISBN 0-8165-0564-0 (bound)   AACR2
ISBN 0-8165-0722-8 (pbk.)

To my muses,
Noah Greenberg
and
Taddeusz Kassern,
in loving memory

Bon ga ureshiya
wakareta hito mo
harete kono yo ni
ai ni kuru

How happy Bon is!
for the departed as well.
Released, they come to This World
to meet us.

"Song for the Festival for Souls," (Fukushima)

Contents

A Word from the Author   ix
How To Pronounce Japanese Words   xii
1. Everybody Sings   1
2. Four Hundred Years of Heroic Virtues   16
3. Folk-Song Poetry   25
4. Types of Japanese Folk Songs   40
5. Musical Accompaniment   66
6. The Present-Day Musical Mixture   84
Discography   89
Bibliography   109
Index   123

Musical Examples

1. "Esashi oiwake" Vocal Score   58
2. Comparative Score: "Fine Fishing Song from Haragama" and "Saitara's Song"   70
3. Comparative Score: "Sōma Barley-hulling Song" and "New 'Song of Sōma'"   72
4. Comparative Score: refrain and *kakegoe* of the "Sōma Mowing Song" and "New 'Song of Sōma'"   73
5. From the "New 'Song of Sōma'"   74
6. "Tsugaru tanto-bushi" Vocal Score   75
7. Examples of *hayashi-kotoba*   77
8. Basic Shamisen Tunings   80
9. "The Factory-girls' Song"   85

In accordance with traditional Japanese practice, Japanese names are written with surnames first, given names last. For many centuries, surnames, in the sense of family or clan names, were reserved for the aristocracy. All others, including artists in various disciplines, were known by given names. To a great extent, this custom has persisted. Thus, the poet Kitahara Hakushū is known as "Hakushū." In the index to this volume, however, the prevailing custom in English-language publishing has been followed and that entry would be "Kitahara, Hakushū."

A Word from the Author

ALMOST EVERY JAPANESE I'VE EVER MET—in Tōkyō, New York, Los Angeles; on the street, in bars, on trains—has enjoyed talking about folk song. Even people who didn't sing or didn't know a particular song would sometimes know something about a song's background. A businessman from Akita was able to explain the local dialect. The owner of a bar knew a few extra wry lines of verse for "Sado okesa." An abstract painter from southern Japan told me the history of Amami-Oshima and when a specific song was popular there.

I have been fascinated with Japanese folk song ever since I stumbled on an American recording of Japanese songs while I was a student at the High School of Performing Arts in New York City. The Japanese words on the record were written in romanization and accompanied by a translation, and I began to learn the fragments of song by rote. I had been brought up on music by major contemporary composers such as Schoenberg, Stravinsky, and Bartok. The vocal techniques and instrumental sounds in the traditional Japanese music seemed extraordinarily modern, and the words were full of wit and emotion. This was incredibly adventurous music.

I became even more attracted to folk song while in college, and especially to the contrapuntal singing, charming poetry, and startling vocal techniques of the Ainu aboriginese of northern Japan. I was inspired to notate their music in detail (until then it had been written down only in outline form).

For some years, the Japanese-American painter and poet, Matsumi Kanemitsu, had encocouraged me to study Japanese in depth. Regarding my desire to be a singer of traditional Japanese songs as perfectly natural, he taught me how to read, write, and speak Japanese whenever he could; loaned me what records he had; and encouraged me to learn and sing songs at Japanese artists' parties in New York and Los Angeles. Eventually I traveled to Japan to research traditional Japanese vocal music, and, as soon as I was settled in Tōkyō, I began looking for folk-song records in department stores and record shops and listening to the Japan Broadcasting Corporation (NHK). The number and variety of beautiful folk songs and superb folksingers far exceeded my expectations.

While doing graduate work, I had seen some of the NHK books of folk songs, including Machida Kashō's and Asano Kenji's *Collection of Japanese Folk Songs (Nihon min'yō-shū)*. At that time, however, I was mainly concerned with finding and learning songs and paid little attention to their historical and cultural backgrounds. In Tōkyō, Mr. Kambayashi Fumio, then of the American Cultural Center, encouraged me to become more conscious of folk-song poetry and the contexts in which the songs are performed. Mr. Kambayashi also introduced me to some of the people at NHK. Mr. Inagaki Tetsurō allowed me to attend several recording sessions at the main NHK building in Tōkyō (at Shibuya), when singers Asari Miki and Satō Matsuko were recording for the New Year's radio folk-song program. At NHK, I also met the great scholar of Japanese folk and popular music, Machida Kashō, who introduced me to the large variety of instruments and instrumental techniques in Japanese folk music.

In Tōkyō and, later, Sōma (Fukashima), I met many other folksingers also, both amateurs and professionals, who sang at parties or in bars. Isaku Matsuzō, my former brother-in-law, would continually call up singers and local scholars and rush me about at all hours on the back of his motorbike to meet them. They would sing and I would listen and make tape recordings of a singer's way of singing a song or his particular voice quality, or I would sometimes chime in with the vocal accompaniments.

When I returned to the States, I was encouraged to continue singing Japanese folk songs—within the tradition, but in my own style. I also continued to study, and I developed even more appreciation of the deep emotion, dialectical nature, and singlemindedness in Japanese music. Even more important, I was brought to the realization that music welcomes enigmas, that the

A Word from the Author

musician doesn't have to explain everything, that, more often than not, music is a private art camouflaged as a public one. This is certainly true of Japanese folk song.

While many people inspired me to write a book on Japanese folk song, special thanks are due to the following for their patient, kind, and courteous help: David P. McAllester, Koizumi Fumio, Mr. and Mrs. Sayanagi Kazuo, Kawase Tadasuke, Ōmura Satoshi, and Oda Tomio; Abiru Hiroka; Ichimura Ayano; Matsumoto Keishin; Hangae Jōsei, Monmoi Kasei, and the Isaku family in Sōma; staff members in charge of folk-song materials at the Japan Broadcasting Corporation (Nippon Hōsō Kyōkai) in Tōkyō; the Japanese and Japanese-American participants in the 1976 Smithsonian Institution's Old Ways in the New World Festival in Washington, D.C.; Mr. Kambayashi Fumio; and Mr. Matsumi Kanemitsu.

Thanks are also due the University of Arizona Press for bringing about publication.

PATIA R. ISAKU

HOW TO PRONOUNCE JAPANESE WORDS

Vowels

Pronounce vowels in a short, clipped manner as follows:

- a   as in father
- i   as in machine
- u   as in Lulu
- e   as in bet
- o   as in horse

When two or more vowels follow each other directly, each retains its original quality and length, but the sequence is pronounced as a continuum, as in ai, au, ie, ue, etc. When the same vowel is repeated directly, it is considered a long vowel and is pronounced as a + a without a break. Long vowels are commonly written as a single letter with a line over them. The most common long vowels are ā, ō, and ū.

Consonants

Before the vowels a, u, e, and o, consonants are hard. Before y and i, they are pronounced as follows:

- by or bi   as "b" in rebuke
- my or mi   as "m" in amuse
- hy or hi   as "h" in humid, etc.

Exceptions are:

- zi   as "j" in reject
- ti   as "ch" in cheap
- tu   as "ts" in tsetse

When two consonants follow each other directly, each retains its original quality and length, as in mi-k-ka.

The letter "r" is not trilled but is pronounced as a cross between "r" and "d," as the word very pronounced with a British accent.

The letter "m" before m, p, or b is pronounced as an m; thus senbei is pronounced sembei, and senmon is pronounced semmon.

Chapter One
Everybody Sings

THE BEAUTIFUL, VAST REPERTOIRE of Japanese folk song, an integral expression of the lively Japanese cultural spirit, is almost unknown in the West.

What is a folk song? Rather, what makes folk songs different from art songs or popular, commercial music? An exact definition is misleading, since any one of the three types of songs can contain elements of the other two. Furthermore, folk song in Japan has always had connections with commercial music through professional entertainers, whether these were outcast beggars or high-ranking performers summoned to amuse the nobility or take part in religious ceremonies. In the long run, it is necessary to accept as folk song whatever the Japanese people themselves consider as such. All the songs discussed in this book are performed at traditional local and national folk festivals, and are recognized as authentic Japanese folk songs by such eminent scholars as Machida Kashō, Takeuchi Tsutomu, and Koizumi Fumio.

Japanese folk songs are composed songs, whether the name of the composers are known or not. But folksingers also improvise music and poetry—with appropriate moods and sentiment—on request, and adapt their songs to a wide variety of performance conditions. They must be able to perform in the middle of a rice field during a planting festival, for instance, or on stage in a theater, or at the Imperial Palace. Therefore, the folksinger must not only be familiar with traditional music, but must be ready to compose and employ new music and musical techniques—by modifying instrumental accompaniment, for example. The folksinger's need to support himself with his singing, to beguile, delight, and move an audience that will pay and shelter him, inspires performers to create and perfect saleable accomplishments. In Japan, folksinging is a skill, a trade.

Yet, folksinging is not limited to professionals alone. Amateurs and semiprofessionals, that is, people who earn their livings from occupations other than singing, form a good part of the folksinging population. Amateur and part-time singers learn by listening to professionals, and professionals get a significant amount of material from amateurs and part-timers.

Folk song is unquestionably a part of the total experience of the Japanese people and an expression of it. Traditional folksinging in Japan belongs to every social class and age group. Many of the greatest singers are people in their seventies, eighties, and even nineties; but children, too, create, maintain, and continually expand their own repertory of folk songs—the *warabe-uta*. Furthermore, unlike some of the other traditional folk-song cultures, there are few restrictions in Japanese folk song that are imposed by the singer's sex; women singers, for instance, are famous for their performances of fiery songs from Hokkaidō and northeastern Japan, men for their performance of geisha songs. (Geisha, literally "artists," are professional girls and women entertainers who are retained for a fee to sing, dance, and recite at big or even small parties. A geisha is not to be confused with a call girl. Geisha songs and song styles are ultrarefined and sophisticated.) The style of a folk song and its demands are far more important than the person who sings it; anyone who can meet a song's demands is welcome to perform it. In other words, a singer's ability is far more important than sex, age, or social status.

Historically, folk song in Japan has never been totally separated from art song and popular song. In fact, *min'yō* (folk song) is a comparatively modern term. Before western musical scholarship and theory influenced Japanese scholars in the late nineteenth century, the enormous repertoire now called folk song was defined and categorized according to the social function of each song, or according to each song's musical or poetic characteristics. Among songpoems dating back to ancient Japan are songs of the seasons, of nature, congratulation songs (such as wedding songs), sacred songs, recollection songs including elegies, songs about personal experiences and feelings, story songs and songs that appeared in stories as commentary or as part of the dialogue, parting songs, travel songs, songs of love in every mood, game songs including songs for wordplay, mourning songs, work songs, beggar-entertainer songs, dialogue songs, insult songs, and incantations. These song forms and themes appear in all Japanese music and poetry, but probably most often in folk song.

The verses of a single songpoem frequently were contributed by different people—a nobleman or court lady, a farmer, a fisherwoman, a professional entertainer, a Shintō shrine-keeper, a Buddhist nun. It was also common practice to quote or allude to verses, lines of verse, or poetic phrases that might be hundreds of years older. This poetic technique is still used in twentieth-century folk-song texts by known authors such as Kitahara Hakushū (1885–1942), who wrote the lyrics for the Shizuoka "Tea-cutters' Song." Many of the songpoems in the *Record of Ancient Matters (Kojiki)* and the *Annals of Japan (Nihon Shoki)* were probably created long before the Nara Period (ca. a.d. 645–ca. 794), when their words were put in writing. The earliest extant anthology of poetry in Japan, the *Collection of a Myriad Leaves (Man'yōshū)* was completed in 759; it contains poems and song texts not only from the Nara Period but from the Suiko Period (ca. 552–ca. 645) and even earlier eras. These practices make it difficult to determine how much of a known author's material is original and how much has come from songpoems that were handed down by word of mouth.

Certain performance and compositional techniques that are typical of Japanese folk song date back to ancient Japan. Among such techniques are the frequent use of mysterious, incomprehensible interjections in a poem; the use of a chorus of voices shouting encouragement to the singer at specified points in a song; the mixture of elevated and vernacular language and imagery; the repetition of lines; the writing of a song text (possibly a skeletal one) as a memory aid for learning and performing the entire song; and the use of variations within basic poetic forms.

In Japan, folk songs are traditionally composed, taught, and learned by ear, that is, worked out formally by oneself or with other people, but not formally on paper. Consequently, children cannot create songs until they have heard many and have had a chance to accumulate a repertoire. Dedicated singers begin to build a repertoire and train their memories while they are still young, so that when they become adults they will have acquired a large enough musical and poetic collection to create additional songs of their own.

Until the late nineteenth and twentieth centuries, the only thing in Japanese folk song that was written down was, on occasion, the song text itself. Memorization and constant practice were essential for composition as well as performance. Even in the 1980s, it is impossible to learn to sing traditional styles of Japanese folk song from music scores alone. As in India, it is essential for the student of folk song to go to a teacher if he wants to learn to sing and play well. Folk-song teachers, formal and informal, can be found everywhere. The primary burden for learning falls on the student, however, and not on the teacher. This burden is not so much one of economics as it is the need for a student to prove the seriousness of his/her intention to learn. His desire to learn has to override every other consideration, because it is so hard to become a good amateur performer, much less a competent artiste.

The Japanese usually withhold some element in a folk song's scoring from most books, including those that use Western notation. If the melodies are included, they aren't detailed; if they are detailed, the vocal accompaniments are left out; if all the words, including the vocal accompaniments, are present, the melodies may not be. Furthermore, books may not give the readings of the lyrics in their local pronunciation or dialect. Therefore, students must listen to established singers to pick up the missing elements.

This lack of detailed notation in folk music is characteristic of the guilds, which were developed in Japan in ancient times to protect the professional secrets of every art from calligraphy to weaving. Lack of detailed notation of a song text protected the traditional teacher, as copyrights protect composers today. (This does not mean that traditional nineteenth- and twentieth-century musicians didn't know and couldn't work with several notations, including Western notations and those of other Japanese schools.) Skeletal notation also helped to give rise to many distinct schools that concentrated on the same, similar, or related pieces, each with its own founder and/or head *(iemoto)*. Basically, each school's variations were the secrets of its teachers and their successful disciples, to be revealed only to their most devoted students.

In any case, no singer can develop properly without hearing many performances of a song and performing it frequently himself. For one thing, performers must become familiar with the Japanese sense of rhythms within the vocal accompaniments (the *kakegoe* and *hayashi*) and the various instrumental accompaniments. For another, they must be able to make musical and historical connections between songs.

It is not easy to become a folksinger, but at parties the Japanese display a generous attitude toward performers. At such occasions, even a tone-deaf businessman will be encouraged to hack his way through a song or poem and will be applauded for his earnest desire to contribute to the fun.

In the *Record of Ancient Matters* (*Kojiki*, completed in 712), joyous music and mirthful dance are associated with the rescue of the world from darkness, panic, and sorrow. The Shintō Sun Goddess, Ama-terasu-ō-mikami, The Great Deity Who Illuminates The Heavens, frightened and angered by the violent acts of the irascible god, her brother Susa-no-wo, shuts herself inside a heavenly cave. The world grows dark, is overrun with disaster and filled with fear. The myriad deities gather. They charge the divine Thought Prince to think. They forge mirrors. They fashion magical curved beads. They tie strips of white and blue cloth to the branches of sacred trees. They establish a harmonious atmosphere before the cave's closed rock door.

Finally, through ecstatic dance, song, and laughter, the deities succeed in luring the Sun Goddess from the cave. Light is restored. Susa-no-wo is cleansed. But, until he redeems himself with noble deeds, he must be banished.

As portrayed in the ancient Japanese chronicles, Susa-no-wo is the antithesis of the traditional artist—not so much because he is a loner and an exile, but because he is the personification of undisciplined emotion. He is happy only after he becomes a serpent-slaying knight errant. Then his violent supernatural actions grow beautiful and creative; from jewels that he chews on, he produces male children. Still, he continues to be associated with the nether world, the pollution of death, and the chaos against which traditional arts have been engaged in combat ever since the creation of the world.

Buddhism was brought to Japan's Imperial Court from China in 552 by way of a Korean embassy and, at the time the *Kojiki* was published, had been accepted by the Japanese people for over a hundred and fifty years. Buddhist beliefs and practices, and earlier beliefs and practices that then came to be defined as Shintō (literally the Way of the Divine), have remained distinct from each other, yet are associated on every level. For instance, the Shintō view of music and dance as depicted in the *Kojiki* is echoed in the folk music and dance of O-Bon, the Japanese Buddhist Festival for Souls.

Buddhism is concerned with the cycle of death and rebirth, and a detachment from worldly cares; and these concerns pervade most narrative songs, as well as all songs of the Festival for Souls. Shintō, on the other hand, comprises the body of Japanese beliefs that involve nature, divinity, and human beings. Shintō manifests itself in folk songs addressed to mountains; in wedding, New Year, and building songs; in farming and fishing songs, and in the fascination with place and season that permeates all Japanese folk-song poetry.

Animism (the belief that the universe itself and everything in it, animate and inanimate, possesses a soul) is expressed in Japanese folk song, too. The folk-song poet personifies such natural phenomena as the seasons, plants, mountains, animals, birds, and fish, addressing them directly to make the personification more emphatic, as in the following examples:

medeta medeta no	O happy, happy
wakamatsu-sama yo	young pine!
eda mo sakaeru	Thy branches flourish!
ha mo shigeru	Thy needles grow luxuriant!

(a stock verse)

Everybody Sings   7

Asama-yama-san
naze yake-shansu
suso ni o-jūroku
mochi-nagara

Mount Asama!
Why are you burning with envy
when you've got
sweet-sixteens at your foot?

"Packhorseman's Song From Komoro" (Nagano)
"Packhorseman's Song From Oiwake" (Nagano)

naku na karasu-ko
sawagu na tombi
orai no warashiga
me o samasu

Don't caw, Crow, honey!
Don't make a racket, Kite!
You'll wake up
our kids!

"The Kanchororin Song" (Fukushima)

    Some of the oldest extant Japanese songpoems are the Blessing Words *(Norito)*. Though Blessing Words were included in the *Kojiki* and other writings of the Nara Period (ca. 645–ca. 794) and early Heian Period (ca. 794–ca. 1185), their exact times of origin are not fully verified, and they may be far older.

    "Norito" is commonly written with the Chinese characters meaning "words that bless; words that felicitate." It has also been written with characters defining the words as ones that purify or exorcise, or as spirit-words—the spirit possibly being one of possession. These Blessing Words are addressed to the divine forces of nature and the cosmos, or come from them through a medium.

    In their oral and written literature the Japanese have always expressed a belief in the supernatural power of words and sound; calling a thing "fortunate" may make it so indeed. Their desire for blessing and purification through word-soul *(koto-dama)* has continued into the twentieth century in many Shintō and Buddhist sacred writings, and in folk song, where it can be seen in the broad category of congratulation songs *(iwai uta)*, in songs celebrating or praying for fine fishing *(tairyō-bushi)*, and in work songs such as rice-planting songs *(ta-ue-uta)* and earth-tamping songs *(do-tsuki-uta)*. The following verse comes from an old congratulation song and is still sung; it illustrates the vitality in this ancient concept of divine intimacy with the arts and divine merriment.

nome ya Daikoku	Drink, O Daikoku, god of wealth!
utae ya Ebisu	Sing, O Ebisu, god of fine fishing!
naka ni shaku toru	Between them,
	the wine-pourer,
Uka-no-kami	the riceplant-force!

"Late Autumn Rain" (Fukushima and Miyagi)

Song-poetry can be associated with and adjusted to individuals, as when a nationally known songpoem is adapted to fit a specific character and location. At the same time, song and dance have always been a major part of community ritual and ceremony in Japan; therefore, most folk songs and dances are designed so that everyone can and will participate. Frequently, verses from the dance songs performed during O-Bon, stress the need for everybody to throw false modesty aside and join in the celebration.

odoru ahō ni	Foolish when you dance,
miru ahō	Foolish when you watch—
onaji aho nara	if you're foolish both ways,
odoran 'ya son son	to not dance is a loss! a loss!

a shout in the "Dance from Awa" (Tokushima)

bon ga kita no ni	Those who won't dance
odoranu mono wa	though the Festival for Souls
	has come
kibutsu kanebutsu	are woodendead Buddhas,
	metaldead Buddhas,
ishibotoke	stonedead Buddhas!

"Bon Song from Sōma" (Fukushima)

The Japanese have always been in love with their folk songs. They sometimes add verses to a song in order to praise it, as in the following examples.

Awa wa yoi toko
Hachisuka-sama no
o-isei odori ni
yo ga akeru

Awa is a splendid place!
The night ends
to Lord Hachisuka's
mighty dance!

"The Dance From Awa" (Tokushima)

kitaru harukaze
kōri ga tokeru
ureshiya kimama ni
owara kiku ume

Comes the next spring breeze,
the ice will melt.
How happy they are!
plum trees
that listen as they please
to the festival song *"owara!"*

"The Owara Song from Etchū" (Toyama)

Or they address a song directly, paying it compliments on its beauty and power.

okuni-jiman no
jongara-bushi yo
wakaishu utatte
aruji no hayashi
musume odoreba
inaho mo odoru

O "Breakdown Song,"
our country's pride!
The young apprentices sing you
to the masters' accompaniment.
When the girls dance to you,
the ears of rice dance, too.

"The Breakdown Song from Tsugaru" (Aomori)

Within one song they may even compose verses advertising another song, as in "The Refrain from Sōma" (Fukushima) or "The Aiya! Song" (Aomori).

ayu wa se ni sumu
tori 'a ki ni tomaru
hito wa nasake no
moto ni yoru
moto ni yoru

Sweetfish live in the shallows.
Birds stay in the trees.
I come close,
come close
to a warm heart.

nihengaeshi de
sumanai naraba
okuni-jiman no
Nagareyama
Nagareyama

If you can't do without
"The Refrain,"
you should hear our country's
  pride,
"The Nagareyama Song!"
"The Nagareyama Song!"

Everybody Sings

Sōma meibutsu	A Sōma specialty:
koma-yaki chawan	the ricebowls with the horse-
	glaze.*
mata mo meibutsu	Still another specialty:
Nagareyama	"The Nagareyama Song,"
Nagareyama	"The Nagareyama Song.
nihengaeshi de	You may do anything twice,
sanbenme ni wa	but the third time,
giri to ninjo no	you're caught;
itabasami	you're caught
itabasami	between Love and Duty.

"The Refrain from Sōma" (Fukushima)

Japanese people sing everywhere—at local festivals, in Tōkoyō bars, at business parties—and traditional folk songs are mingled with old popular songs, school songs, western songs, or the latest hits.

Local songs often become well known throughout the country, but usually in an altered form. Therefore, to appreciate a song fully, it is necessary to go to its birthplace and hear it sung within its own communal and individual surroundings—in its own climate, and under its own skies—since local and regional dialects, festivals, customs, ways of expressing emotion, and differences in the way people look and dress are still very distinctive. In the twentieth century, there are at least fifty places that are nationally famous for their folk songs. Indeed, love of and pride in a place pervade Japanese folk-song poetry. Verse after verse dwell on the distinctive character and beauties of a local spot. A sense of place and season is full of poignancy to the folk-song poet, as it is to the writer of *haiku*. This feeling is echoed in the phrase *furusato no uta* (songs from back home). *Furusato* literally means "old village." It is a word full of nostalgia and is frequently used in titles of folk-song records, books, and radio and television programs on folk song.

*Sōma is famous for its glazed pottery, which always features the picture of a horse. "Sōma" means "to tell the good points of a horse."

During the Tokugawa Period, from the 1640s to the 1860s, except for those provinces in the deep south which carried on a sporadic, half-clandestine trade with China and, through Dutch traders, with Europe, Japan was shut off from the world outside. Nevertheless, the Japanese traveled about on their own islands, as if they were visiting foreign countries. Travelers carried their local songs with them and took new songs home as souvenirs.

Izumo meibutsu	Izumo Province's specialty
nimotsu ni'a naranu	won't weigh your luggage down.
kiite okaeri	You hear it, you take it home:
Yasugi-bushi	the "Song from Yasugi."

"Song from Yasugi" (Shimane)

The transplanted song would often take on a new form, or give birth to a new song, as the "It-cha-It-cha Song" from Chiba did when it became the ancestor of the Fukushima "Song of Sōma" and the relative of the "Niishima It-cha Song" (Tōkyō Municipality). ("It-cha-It-cha" is an interjection, like "Hey nonny-nonny!")

Verses that have become so popular they can't be confined to a single place, song, or song genre but travel from one to another are common, too. Folk-song poets often compose variations on such traveling verses, or on individual lines of verse. (The authors of the following examples are unknown, but these lines and verses appear in other songs also.)

kokoro-bososa ni	As in heart's loneliness
yamaji o yukeba	I go along the mountain roads,
kasa ni ko no ha wa	leaves come dancing down
mai-kakaru	on my hat of bamboo.

"Sōma Packhorseman's Song" (Fukushima)

kokoro-bosoi yo	My heart is lonely!/I'm lonely!/
	It's lonely!
yamaji o yukeba	As I go along the mountain roads

"Song of Kiso" (Nagano)

12   *Everybody Sings*

ayu wa se ni tsuku tori 'a ki ni tomaru hito wa nasake no moto ni sumu	The sweetfish reach the shallows; birds rest in the trees; we live under your compassion.

"The Barley-and-Such Song" (Toyama)

hito wa nasake no kage ni sumu	I live beneath the shade of your love.

"The Packhorseman's Art Song from Esashi" (Hokkaidō)

From traveling verses come stock lines and epithets, which are as important in Japanese folk-song poetry as they are in the poetry of other cultures. The Japanese son or daughter who is "raised like a butterfly, a flower" is certainly akin to Homer's "winedark sea" or the British "milk-white steed."

chō yo hana yo to **sodateta** musume	Our daughter, **raised** **like a butterfly!** **a flower!**
chō yo hana yo to **sodateru** uchi ni	While he's being **brought up** **like a butterfly!** **a flower!**
sorota sorota yo wakaishu ga **sorota**	**All present!** **All present!** (The boys) are **all present!**
sorota sorota yo odoriko **sorota**	**Ready! Ready!** (The dancing-girls) are **all ready!**

Besides using stock lines and stock phrases, some poets also develop verses with related phrases, ideas, *and themes*. From

kokoro-boso a ni yamaji o yukeba kasa ni ko no ha wa mai-kakaru	As in heart's loneliness I go along the mountain road, leaves come dancing down on my hat of bamboo.

(traveling verse)

may come

kokoru-sabishiya
bakuro no yomichi
naru wa kutsuwa no
oto bakari

Ah, how lonely it is!
a lowly packhorseman's
    night road,
the jangling bit
the only sound...

(traveling verse)

or

kokoro-sabishiya
ochiyuku michi wa
kawa no naruse to
shika no koe

Ah, how lonely they are!
On the escape route,
the roar of the rapids,
and the deer's voices...

"The Barley-and-Such Song" (Toyama)

Japanese folk songs are frequently known by their place of origin—"The Lullaby From Itsuki Village," "An Akita Miller's Song." In Japan, folk songs have been used to promote public relations for well over four hundred years. Groups of people need to put themselves on a map, to tell the world about their province, their town, their village, their hot springs resort or harbor. A familiar line in folk song is

A–B wa yoi toko
A–B–C yoi toko*

X is a nice place!"

often followed by

ichido wa oide
ichido wa gozare

Do come at least once!

*Depending on the song's mood, *yoi* can be translated as "beautiful," "fine," "splendid," "lovely," "good," or "wonderful."

An equally familiar verse is

ano yama takakute	That mountain is high,
[chimei] (wa) mienu	and I can't see [place name].
[chimei] koishiya	How I love [place name]!
yama nikuya	How I hate the mountain!

There are some towns that are famous for only one or two folk songs, as Shimoda (Shizuoka) is known for the "Shimoda Song," while others, such as Sōma (Fukushima), are renowned for as many as ten or twenty. National recognition, however, is no indication of the number of local songs that originate in a place. An area may be full of songs, but only one or two gain a national audience. The important thing is to gain recognition and then keep it.

The word most often used by the Japanese to describe Japanese folk song, referring both to its language and music, is "difficult." The physical and technical challenges of the songs delight audiences as well as performers. So does the language of folk-song poetry, with its mixture of the delicate and vulgar, of wit and emotion, of the secular and religious.

Japanese folksingers regard their songs as a source of pride and comfort. Whether it is a rice-planting song, a factory worker's song, or a geisha song, each piece has two styles: its own and that of the genre to which it belongs. Like jazz singers and those of German lieder, Japanese singers will study selected folk songs for years in order to perfect their comprehension and performance.

Most Japanese folksingers know in detail the oral history of every song they perform. Folk-song students learn to trace musical and textual connections between one song and another just by hearing the songs; then they consult other singers, books, or recordings to find what connections do indeed exist, and the history of these connections. It is not uncommon for a Japanese folksinger to know several different versions of the same song and to launch into an involved technical discussion, complete with vocal and instrumental comparisons. This is true not only of professional and semiprofessional singers, but of amateurs, aficionados, and members of the audience. They all follow every psychological nuance, every use of local dialect and pronunciation, every epigram, every word game. In Japan, appreciating folk songs is a lifelong enterprise.

Chapter Two
Four Hundred Years of Heroic Virtues

MANY JAPANESE FOLK SONGS that are performed today date from the sixteenth century.

In 1518, toward the end of the Muromachi Period (ca. 1392–ca. 1573), an unknown author, possibly a Buddhist monk, published the *Kanginshū (Anthology of Leisure Recitations)*, a collection of three hundred and eleven popular folk-song texts. Consisting largely of *ko-uta*, the short lyric songs then fashionable, the *Kanginshū* also included longer jugglers' songs; some Chinese-style intoned poems; banquet songs *(enkyoku);* songs associated with Nō drama and Kyōgen farce, both patronized by the nobility; local songs from Ōmi and Yamato, provinces near Kyōto, the capital; and some early songs that were part of the *dengaku*, the rice-field-planting-festival music and dance. (Later, during the Tokugawa Period [ca. 1603–ca. 1868], *dengaku* also became Shintō shrine music.) A separate collection of songs from the rice-planting festivals, the *Ta-ue-zōshi (Copybook of Rice Planting)*, was published at about the same time.

When these songbooks appeared, rival clans had been waging larger and larger territorial wars within Japan for some fifty years. Warfare and shifts of power continued until the Tokugawa family gained control of the country in the early 1600s. Despite the chaos of the age, however, this was also a time of lively cutural growth throughout Japan, with the mercantile and artisan classes beginning their slow, perilous rise as a social-artistic force. Commoners became the supporters of art forms that were to flourish in the Tokugawa Period, such as the doll-puppet theater (the Bunraku), the Kabuki theater, the wood-block print, the novel, and a multitude of new and older popular song styles. In the 1560s, the shamisen was introduced into Japan from the Ryūkyū Islands. Unlike most of the instruments then in Japan, the shamisen had had a totally secular, totally disreputable history in China and the Ryūkyūs, where it was the instrument of the theater, the red-light district, the vagabond. The Japanese people embraced it wholeheartedly, and it soon became an essential accompaniment to popular songs. From the seventeenth century on, the shamisen accompanied the doll-theater's narrator and was a chief instrument in the Kabuki theater orchestra.

Technically, the shamisen proved to be a most flexible instrument. It can be played with a plectrum or, for some kinds of music, with the fingernail of the index finger. And it is collapsible and can be easily carried in a small case. It comes in all sizes for all types and moods of music—from the subtle, muted accompaniment of geisha songs to flashy Kabuki theater music to the ornamented fury of Tsugaru folk songs. However, Japanese performers found the shamisen's original snakeskin body too brittle for their passionate temperaments. Eventually they changed to the more flexible skins of the cat, dog, and raccoon-like creature, the *tanuki*.* The shamisen craze swept the country, and, over three hundred years later, it remains one of the most popular instruments in Japan; shamisen-accompanied songs make up at least a third of the folk-song repertoire alone.

In the 1590s, book printing was reintroduced into Japan from Korea and given new impetus. Inexpensive editions of religious and secular classics soon became available and were welcomed by a wide audience. This encouraged the publication of other books, including song books, for the instruction and amusement of all social classes. Among these new works were the *Muneyasu*

---

*As inquisitive as its relative the raccoon, which it resembles, the *tanuki* is attracted to human beings. The Japanese are charmed and amused by the creature, about whom they have invented a whole body of folk literature.

In Japanese folklore, the *tanuki* embodies the joys of wine, sex, feasting, music, and dance. It is fond of changing its shape and creating magical illusions.

The *tanuki* is principally associated with the shamisen and with drums; as they dance, so the story goes, *tanuki* accompany themselves by drumming on their bellies, which produces a pleasing, shamisen-like sound. There are a number of *tanuki* folk songs and dances, including the "Raccoon Dance" of Kagawa Prefecture.

Anthology of Airs (Muneyasu ko-uta-shū) by Kuga Yūan Sankyū, and *Ryūtatsu's Anthology of Airs (Ryūtatsu ko-uta-shū)* by Kozambo Jian Ryūtatsu; probably both compilers were Buddhist monks. Other collections of folk songs appeared with increasing regularity during the Tokugawa Period.

The Tokugawa Period appears peaceful, compared with preceding decades when clan wars continually passed the reins of government from one family to another. And yet, it was an age of peasant revolts; more than eighty such insurrections were taken seriously enough to be documented, including the traumatic uprising at Shimabara in 1637. All through this era, the clash between ordinary human feelings and the noble Confucian ideal of overwhelming moral-social obligation affected the shape and content of the popular art forms. According to the Neo-Confucian outlook of the time, the peasants were the virtuous class; then came the nobles and warriors; then finally the merchants and artisans—who were considered lacking in virtue.

Therefore, despite their popularity with the public, the new Tokugawa art forms were resented by central administrators, who regarded them as an upstart display of luxury, an unhealthy fascination with the novel, and an undermining of the proper order of things. The administrators thought the artists willfully created and romanticized conflicts between *giri* (duty; obligation) and *ninjō* (human nature; human feelings). It irritated the central government that the plebeian Kabuki and Bunraku theaters depicted and occasionally influenced current events, and that samurai (warriors) and noblemen, who should have remained aloof from disreputable classes and interests, often patronized merchants and artists, and even mingled with them. The shogunate (military government) chafed when the arts portrayed merchants and courtesans as people who were moved by the same sentiments and who possessed the same virtues as the nobly born.

For example, during the Tokugawa Period, the shogunate was disconcerted when many women in red-light districts, unable to quit the prostitute's life and marry, or unable to escape from their financial entanglements, committed suicide with their lovers. Since ancient times in Japan, suicide had been the noble's way to counteract defeat. Now, all at once, the knightly code of honor was being perversely embraced by persons of the lowest degree. Double love-suicides came to be known as *shinjū* (the inner heart and mind), but during the reign of the Kyōhō-era Emperor

(1716-1735), Judge Ōoka Echizen-no-kami decided that *shinjū*, if read backwards, would be *chūshin* (loyalty). He declared it ridiculous to call a double love-suicide an act of loyalty. Certainly the lovers had not been loyal to their castes. The Judge ordered such suicides to be called Death by Mutual Consent.* But, while the expression Death by Mutual Consent may have been used in official documents, it was never adopted by the people. To this day, *shinjū*, with its connotations of loyalty and sincerity, is the popular word for double love-suicides.

Although an unemployed and debt-ridden warrior class and an aristocracy almost completely out of touch with contemporary society remained in power over the increasingly energetic and aggressive merchant class which had assumed many of the stoic samurai virtues, all through this period there was an irrepressible exchange of arts among the classes. Wealthy merchants' daughters studied the aristocratic Nō drama or the tea ceremony. Samurai became proficient on the Chinese violin. Accomplished courtesans learned and performed the songs that working-class folk brought with them from their old homes. Respected scholars and Buddhist monks turned to publishing collections of popular folk songs, putting themselves in the company of gay-quarter habitués and low-class characters like Bazan the Woodchopper (Bazan Shōfu), the eighteenth-century author of *Woodchopping Folk Songs (Shōso fūzoku uta*, published ca. 1770). (The monks were simply living up to their age-old reputation in Japan for passionate embroilment in the most worldly concerns.) In fact, the scholars of the day produced most of the extant collections from the late Muromachi and Tokugawa Periods. The late-Tokugawa artist and scholar Kodera Gyokuchō published at least three collections of folk songs between 1834 and 1847. If the songs in Gyokuchō's *Ballads-and-Airs Scene (Ko-uta no chimata)* and his other works do not sufficiently express the anxieties and hardships of an entertainer's life (the novels of the seventeenth century author Ihara Saikaku give a fuller picture), they do show the skill, elegance, and beauty that folksingers and their audiences required of their lyricists. Twentieth-century scholars of Japanese folk song, such as Machida Kashō and Takeda Chūichirō have kept up this tradition and have contributed new songs to the national repertoire. Machida is the

*DeBecker, J. E., *Yoshiwara, The Nightless City*, Reprint of Third Edition (1905), (New York: Frederick Publications, 1960), p. 184.

composer of "The Tea-cutters' Song" of Shizuoka Prefecture, and Takeda wrote the music and words of the "New 'Late Autumn Rain'" of Miyago.*

The Tokugawa scholars may have been inspired by the revered composers and compilers of songpoems in the ancient Chinese *Book of Songs (Shr jing)* and its later Japanese offshoot, the *Collection of a Myriad Leaves (Man'yōshū)*. These earlier Chinese scholar-poets, and the more daring Chinese historians, had depicted every level of their contemporary society, using the language, poetry, and songs of courtesans, entertainers, and bandits, as well as the idiom of the Imperial Court or the style of the Imperial Academy. In the centuries that followed, Chinese scholar-novelists and scholar-dramatists, and Japanese scholar-artists, continued in their example, producing books of new folk songs.

Recurrently through the Tokugawa Period, the central administration tried to curb signs of restlessness and the dangerous mixture of classes by issuing edicts restricting travel, forbidding social intermingling, limiting the number of theaters and publishing houses, prohibiting the study of the arts of one class by members of another, and regulating matters of dress. However, rather than constricting activity in the arts, the edicts seemed to promote even more defiance and creativity.

As so often happens when governments attempt to stifle political and social freedom, people seek release through new ideas and new art forms. In the Tokugawa Period, the poor farmer, the harried noble, the often abused itinerant musician, as well as the respected artist living on local or central government rice revenues, gained a sense of human dignity by singing about defeated and beloved heroes of Japanese history, the beauty of the surroundings, love and longing for home and family. The artists of the period reacted to social and political pressures by developing new artistic skills and disciplines. A cult of "singlemindedness" developed, with discipline implying a high level of individual responsibility (the practice of noble virtues) and the willingness to spend an entire lifetime in pursuit of one goal. For example, groups of musicians would devote all their energies to perfecting a particular style of music, and would

*See the notes on "Shin sansa shigure" ("New 'Late Autumn Rain'") in the booklet that is included with the record album, *Tōhoku min'yō daizenshū* (Nippon Columbia), p. 45.

search through an endless variety of styles to find the one to which they were willing to give permanent loyalty. Artists' guilds, schools, and styles that arose during the Tokugawa Era have modern offshoots that continue to observe traditional obligations. The same samurai code of honor that influenced Tokugawa artists still governs modern Japanese artists in their search for a teacher. A special loyalty develops between these teachers and their disciples, who become lifelong members of a school-family. This tie to a particular school or teacher has a powerful hold on many contemporary artists, who otherwise appear to have few or no connections with the past.

The concept of singlemindedness is as variable as the infinite number of divisions and subdivisions within the arts and crafts pictured in Tokugawa wood-block prints. Some folksingers perform only songs of their hometown or region, as do Momonoi Kasei and the Hangae family of Sōma (Fukushima), Asari Miki of the Tsugaru region in Aomori, Natsuzaka Kikuo of the Nambu region in Aomori-Iwate, and Ōshima O-Riki of Ōshima Island (Tōkyō Municipality). Other singers perform only one song—such as the "Ballad From Kawachi" (Ōsaka) or the "Ballad From Ōmi" (Shiga)—albeit with a variety of texts. This tendency to specialize extends to instrumental accompaniment also. Some folksingers use western orchestral arrangements almost exclusively; others use only Japanese instruments. All these performers are maintaining an ancient heritage to a greater or lesser degree.

On the other hand, there are many respected performers, regarded as authentic folksingers, who also perform traditional or modern music, and there are singers who include a variety of songs from different locales in their repertoires. Ko-uta Katsutarō, born in Niigata Prefecture and one of the great geisha singers, has recorded popular songs, Niigata folk songs, and a popular type of late-Tokugawa art song, the *ha-uta*. Mihashi Michiya, a Tsugaru-style shamisen player, sings popular songs and, usually, orchestra-accompanied folk songs. Kishi Yōko is a French style chanteuse who also sings folk songs (such as "Shōnai Belle") from Yamagata, her home prefecture. She sometimes sings, too, one of the modern popular songs in a heavy Yamagata accent, which brings down the house. Tsunoda Masataka concentrates on folk songs from his two homes, Akita Prefecture and Hokkaidō. And, although not a geisha, Satō

Matsuko sings songs from many prefectures in a geisha-cum-Kabuki-theater style, as they are performed at traditional banquets and parties all over the country. A favorite theme in Japanese fiction, dama, and movies is the heroic effort of the individual artist—actor, calligrapher, painter, tea-maker, dancer, swordfighter, singer—to demonstrate singlemindedness in pursuit of his beloved art. It is this proof of dedication that enables a student to begin the long, demanding apprenticeship under a teacher, to learn the mysteries of the school or style, and, in the ripeness of time, to create mysteries for his own disciples to inherit, maintain, and build upon.

Before the Tokugawa Period, the awarding of a nom d'artiste *(geimei)* had been a common practice among professional Japanese artists for about five hundred years. In addition to their original names, almost all artists were awarded at least one other name associated with some aspect of their professional progress. Some artists acquired as many as three or more different names. This custom continues, as in the names inherited by Kabuki actors when they reach the highest point of their careers— "Nakamura Utaemon" for the player of young heroines, "Ichikawa Danjūrō" for the player of flamboyant strong men, and so on. Professional names confer an identity and often signify a major change for the better in the life of their users.

From the Tokugawa Period through the present, professional folksingers have had disciples who eventually adopted or were awarded their teachers' full names, surnames, or syllables from their names. Among contemporary examples are the late Hamada Kiichi and his younger brother and heir, Hamada Kiichi; Minemura Toshimisa and her disciples Minemura Toshiko and Minemura Toshimatsuwaka; Sugimoto Shūchō, head of the Horiuchi school or style of folk singing in Sōma, and fellow members Endo Shūrei and Abe Shūrō, who are also well-known singers. (Some Sōma folk songs have northern and southern versions; the Horiuchi school is concerned with northern styles. The school is probably named after Horiuchi Hidenosuke, a Sōma folksinger, composer, and teacher. The Sino-Japanese reading of the first character in "Hidenosuke" is "shū"; therefore Horiuchi-school names, at least for one generation, all contain that character with that reading.) Professional singers also adopt a variety of art surnames. They may use the names of their homes (as does **ōshima** O-Riki), their professional homes (as **akasaka** Ko-ume took her name from the Akasaka district in Tōkyō), or the names of particular kinds of songs. For example, the *ko-uta* (a little song, an air) is a song style that dates back to the late Muromachi period, and Ko-uta is a popular art surname for geisha. Geisha folksingers can often be recognized as such by their professional names. They may take the name of a district famous for its geisha, such as Shimbashi or Akasaka, for their surnames, and use the masculine name or name suffix *tarō* in their first names, as do Katsu**tarō** and Kiku**tarō**. Many geisha use this masculine name, or take other four-to-six syllable first names, masculine style. Such names underline the geisha's status as an artist, and thus the difference of her life from that of the average Japanese woman. (An ordinary woman's name in Japan is never longer than three syllables.) A masculine name also adds the charm of contrast to a geisha's studied feminity.

Groups of folksingers sometimes name themselves after particular songs, too, as did the Etchū Gokayama "mugi ya-bushi" hozon-kai (The Etchū Province Gokayama Village "Barley-and-Such Song" Conservation Society),* or take their names from lines of verse in a song. A group that performs the "Ballad from Aikawa" and other Sado Island folk songs from Niigata calls itself The Rising Waves Society (Tatsunami-kai), from the lines

dot-to warōte	A burst of laughter
tatsunami kaze no	in that wild movement of
araki orifushi . . .	**the rising waves** and
	wind . . .

"Ballad from Aikawa" (Aikawa)

*This group sings folk songs from Toyama Prefecture, including a "Long Version of the 'Barley-and-Such Song.'"

But names don't go just from songs to singers but from singers to songs also; a folk song named after a singer usually takes the first name of its singer-composer. (Until the late nineteenth century in Japan, surnames were the exclusive property of the upper classes.) Some of the most famous examples of singer-composers' names as song titles are "Kenryō's Song" (Aomori; the composer's name was Matsuzaki Kenryō); the group of dance songs known as *okesa*, after the geisha on Sado Island who is said to have composed the first of these songs many hundreds of years ago; and "Saitara's Song" (Miyagi; the composer was a foundryman turned fisherman).

The artistic life-style in Japan applies to women as well as men. The history of women artists in China and Japan is long and impressive. Happily, there is a large body of Chinese and Japanese literature that portrays many of these extraordinary people.

As performers master a particular genre or style, they become creatively involved with the music and poetry and begin to develop their own ornamentation—additions to or variations on the melody, the accompaniments, or lyrics; or preferences for particular melodic or textual versions. Once he or she becomes creatively involved, the performer often composes pieces of his own, which he in turn contributes to the repertoire. Singer Suzuki Masao composed the "New 'Song of Sōma,'" while the *shakuhachi* player Narita Un'chiku created the "Apple Song" (Aomori).

Scholars of Japanese folk song have also created songs. Machida Kasho is the composer of "The Tea-cutting Song" of Shizuoka Prefecture; Takeda Chuichiro composed the music and words of the "New 'Late Autumn Rain'" of Miyagi.

There is continuous creation also through the syntheses of earlier and modern genres and styles. This dynamic process, this simultaneous blending of the traditional and contemporary, is still manifested, however, in the Japanese aesthetic of singlemindedness and lifelong adherence to one's group.

Chapter Three
Folk-Song Poetry

IN SOME COUNTRIES, THE LYRICS OF A SONG are much more important than its music; in others, the music is far more important than the words. In France, for example, the melodies of many songs have little variety; all the emphasis is on the lyrics. In Italy, on the other hand, much of the operatic libretti seems secondary; the music is everything. In Japan, words and music are so interdependent that since ancient times a single word, *uta*, has always meant both poem and song.

In ancient Japan, poetry was intoned, much as the eighth-century *tanka* (short poem) and the fifteenth-century Nō drama still are. But when *tanka* were sung outright, that is, set to a melody, they became part of a song genre, the *rōei*, which dates from the Heian Period (ca. 794–ca. 1185) and is still performed. *Rōei* (melodious recitation) style and content reflect knightly sentiments and the genre includes the singing in Japanese of short Chinese poems. The term *rōei* also refers to a *tanka* when it is sung rather than intoned.

Tanka may also be called *waka* (Japanese poems) to distinguish them from *kanshi* (Chinese poems). The singing of *kanshi* in Japanese translation grew into another song genre of the nineteenth and twentieth centuries, known as *shigin* (the recitation of Chinese poetry). *Kanshi* have been performed as a summons to battle and as a call to peace. They are sung by both men and women, many of whom also sing epics and accompany themselves on the *biwa*, an instrument directly developed from the Chinese pear-shaped lute, the *pipa*.

Waka and *kanshi* are often performed together, providing subtle but dramatic contrasts in musical and poetic style. A significant number of *kanshi* written by Japanese poets incorporate examples of other Japanese vocal genres ranging from Nō drama to folk song. There are also combinations of speaking, intoning, and singing in poetic drama, as in the doll-puppet theater and the nineteenth- and twentieth-century popular folk mono-drama, the *naniwa-bushi* (music from Naniwa [modern Osaka]).

Throughout the recorded history of China and Japan, there have been government officials who were also poets. For centuries, the administrations of both countries considered contemporary folk-song poetry an infallible gauge of public opinion on local and national affairs. Therefore, thorough scholars included the folk-song poetry of the period in their histories, topographies, memoirs, and state documents. The title of a twentieth-century collection by Kubo Kenwo, *A Topography of Children's Songs from Southern Japan (Minami Nihon warabe-uta fudoki)*, refers directly to this practice.

But folk-song poetry is not only thought of as a source of historical, anthropological, or topical information. The subject matter, language, and forms of Japanese folk-song poetry have attracted and inspired even avant-garde writers like Kitahara Hakushū (1885–1942), who is known in the West for dazzling poems such as "Secret Music of Heresy" and "Okaru-Kampei." Periodically, Hakushū also wrote lyrics for new folk songs and for children's school songs.

Hakushū was following the lead of a diverse group of classical writers which included the Han Dynasty Chinese historian Sze-ma Chyen, the Tang Dynasty poets Li Po, Tu Fu, and Li Ho, Ching Dynasty Chinese novelist Tsao Swe-chin, and, from Japan, Heian Period novelist Lady Murasaki and Tokugawa novelist Ihara Saikaku. All felt it necessary to incorporate folk-song poetry into their work, no matter how remote their own day-to-day experiences were from those farmers, fishers, vendors, artisans, beggars, or call girls who had first composed the songs. Folk and popular singers repaid the compliment with performances of the writers' songs and dramatizations of their stories.

The local folk-song poets today, though living far from the acknowledged centers of refined culture, continue to use the language and subject matter of urban writers to enhance their works, as they did in the past. In Japanese, for instance, a verb does not merely describe an action; a verb itself indicates the doer's age, sex, social status, and temperament. If you are my superior, in Japanese, "you eat" is *"meshiagarimasu"*; "I eat" is *"itadakimasu."* If you are my equal, "you eat" is *"tabemasu,"* and so is "I eat." If you are my inferior or an animal, however, "you eat" is *"kuu,"* especially if I am angry at you, and "I eat" is *"taberu"* or *"morau."* The "Ballad from Aikawa," a song that describes the land and sea battles of two rival clans, gains much of its powerful effect through the use of the most dignified verb forms for the noble hero; even in the heat of hand-to-hand combat, he "deigns to spur" his horse into the waves.

There are over thirty ways in Japanese of saying the word "you," each with its own social and emotional context and implications. Many of these words for "you" have other meanings that occasionally give them an air of remoteness and courtesy, which is comforting to the ardent but shy Japanese:

omae	the one present, the one facing me (you)
o-nushi	the owner, master (you)
nushi	one's husband; also implies "my dear," "my lover" (you)
anata	the place of honor (you)
kimi	lord, lady, prince(ss), monarch (you)

In some contexts, saying "you" directly *("anata," "anta," "kimi")* is tantamount to a declaration of love, intimacy, or informality. In other contexts, direct address is the equivalent of an insult or a challenge to fight: *"kisama"* ("You _____!"). The various meanings of Japanese words for "you," with their greater and lesser degrees of familiarity, depend on the historical era, place, person, etc.

One of the most impressive examples of the use of language to identify a specific person occurred in a period movie, in which one of the characters, who belonged to a gang of spies, tried to disguise himself by using a samurai word, *"sessha,"* for "I." When the heroine failed to be taken in, he "removed" his disguise by changing his "I" back to *"ore,"* that of a desperado. Such subtleties in colloquial Japanese and their apparently endless number fascinate and bewilder most westerners and cause the Japanese themselves to admit—with pride—that their language, like their folk song, is "difficult." In the spoken language, too, there are words that represent punctuation marks—which confuses many westerners even more. For example,

"Zo," "yo," or *"ya"* implies an exclamation point.

    nome ya   Drink!
    tanomu yo I'm counting on you!
    abunai zo Look out! (*"Zo"* is normally used
                        by men only).

"Ka" signifies a question mark. (Women often say "Sō ja nai no"— *"no"* being a gentler equivalent of *"ka."* This *"no"* should not be confused with the possessive particle.)

    sō ja nai ka   Right?

"Yo" or *"ya"* after a noun implies the vocative "O" or "Ah."

    jongara-bushi yo   O Breakdown Song!

    furuike ya   Ah, you poor old pond!
    kawazu tobikomu frogs jumping in,
    mizu no oto   water-racket...

                                                        a haiku *by Bashō*

"X ya Y" means "X and/or Y."

"Ya" after an adjective or stative verb translates as "How _____ !" or "It's so _____ !"

    shiorashiya   It's so lovely!

Folk-song poets use such punctuation words when they want to stress a mood or make the punctuation unequivocally clear. However, it is also possible both in colloquial speech and in poetry to imply a question or an exclamation without punctuation words. Within a certain context, the tone of voice, and more concretely, verb endings such as *"—nu"* emphasize the distinctions (*"—nu"* indicates an abrupt negative that would be followed by an exclamation point in English, as in *"konu"* ["I won't come!"]). Due to the flexibility of the Japanese language, the same lines of verse can be an extended adjectival construction, a prepositional phrase after the predicate, or the subject and predicate before the object.

> Bitchū Takahashi
> Matsuyama odori
> tsuki no e ni naru
> oshiro no yaba de
>
> *"The Matsuyama Dance" (Okayama)*

can mean either

> On the castle archery ground,
> where the Matsuyama Dance
> of Takahashi in Bitchū Province
> becomes a picture in the moonlight, ...

or

> The Matsuyama Dance
> of Takahashi in Bitchū
> becomes a picture in the moonlight
> on the castle archery ground.

or both at once.

Often one word with multiple meanings will give multiple feelings to a single verse.

> Usui-tōge no
> Gongen-sama wa
> NUSHI no tame ni wa
> mamori-gami
>
> *"Packhorseman's Song from Oiwake" (Nagano)*

can mean

> Lord Gongen, the Boddhisatva
> of Usui Pass,
> is **my lover's**
> guardian god.

or

> . . .
> is **my master's**
> guardian god.

or

> . . .
> is **your**
> guardian god.

Ellipsis, the omission in a phrase or sentence of words which are implied or understood, is also common in Japanese speech and poetry. The English "Well! I never!" is multiplied and developed a thousandfold.

| uchi no oyadachi'a | My parents |
| nero nero to | (are saying) "Sleep! Sleep!" |

"Sōma Barley-hulling Song" (Fukushima)

| ima wa Koshiji no | Now (they wear) Koshiji |
| soma-gatana | woodcutters' knives. |

"The Barley-and-Such Song" (Toyama)

| oyama wa yuki yo | The mountain is |
| | (covered with) snow! |

"Zarantoshō (Miyagi)"

Often this brevity of expression leads to terse poetic sketches of great beauty, akin to those in some classical Chinese poetry. Ellipsis can also lead to different meanings within a verse or can produce startling metaphors. Because of the omission of a specific grammatical particle, the verse

> Ah, how lonely they are!
> **on the escape route,**
> the roar of the rapids,
> and deer's voices...

can also be understood to mean

> Ah, how lonely they are!
> **the escape route is**
> the roar of the rapids,
> and deer's voices.
>
> (kokoro sabishiya
> ochiyuku michi wa
> kawa no naruse to
> shika no koe)

"The Barley-and-Such Song" (Toyama)

When the poet who composed the following lines for the "Packhorseman's Art Song From Esashi" (Hokkaidō) sings of the sadness of lovers parting, the words have all the more emotional force because of their lack of a specific reference—in the Japanese verse, there is no subject in the first clause, and, depending on who is singing, the word *"hito"* (person) in the second line can mean "I," "he," "she," and, by implication, "you."

naita tote	Though (blank) cried,
dōse yuku hito	anyway, the person
	who is going
yaraneba naranu	must be allowed to go.

Folk-Song Poetry

can mean either

> though you cried,
> you have to
> let me leave.

or

> though we cried,
> I have to
> let you leave.

or

> she cried!
> still, he
> must go.

or

> he cried!
> still, she
> must go.

However, even though in the Japanese verse one subject is omitted and the other is open to interpretation, the emotion is specific, and the singer is free to apply it to himself, herself, or others.

Like the dramatists of the doll-puppet theater and the kabuki theater, Japanese folk-song poets are fond of epigrammatical conceits, metaphors, playing upon words, hidden meanings, dual and even contradictory meanings, and parody.

Contradiction, dualism, or dialectic often arise in Japanese folk-song poetry, when, for example, tender thoughts are expressed in terrifying imagery.

yama wa yakete mo	Even if the mountain is burning down,
yamadori'a tobanu	the mountain birds won't fly away!
kawai wagako ni	enthralled
hikasarete	by my darling child...

"*Grain-pounding Song from Awa*" *(Tokushima)*

This verse can also be translated

> Even if the mountain is burning,
> the mountain birds won't fly away!
> Drawn
> to our beloved children...

or

> Even if the mountain is burning,
> I, a mountain bird,
> won't fly away! Drawn
> to my beloved children...

Because of the variety of meanings and moods that are attainable, some of the narrative folk songs in Japan become excellent subjects for musical and poetical parody. One version of the "Ballad from Omi" (Shiga) is a takeoff on a familiar kind of narrative folk song that has an elaborate introduction and slow buildup to the climax. In this version, the singer leads the audience to expect a terrific fight scene, then sabotages the expectation by informing everyone that our hero's sword is made of bamboo.* In a savagely comical parody on the "Song from Yagi" (Gumma and Tochigi), the hero is not the brave gambling boss of the original but a harassed Tokyo businessman —one not being sung about, but singing about himself. The music, too, is a parody of itself. Instead of a fierce small solo flute, there is an accordion; the honking of the sake cask fades to the *sh-sh* of a

---

*This version is recorded on *Nihon no min'yō*, Side 13, Item #118; performed by Gōshu Yasunori/Ando (the soloist's art name) with Sakuragawa Umeo and his troupe.

snare drum; the singer's voice, rather than resembling a wolf at full howl, takes on a diffident Tin Pan Alley lilt.*

Verses that say one thing but mean something in addition have also been accepted for centuries in Japanese society and politics as a legitimate expression of a singer's true thoughts and emotions. The verse that follows

mugi ya natane wa	Though you reap barley, rape, and such
ninen de karu ni	after two years,
asa ga kararyo ka	how can you bear to cut
handoyo ni	the young flax halfway through the summer days

Barley-and-Such Song (Toyama)

is a metaphorical expression of compassion for the young boys who died in battle in the twelfth-century wars between the Minamoto and Taira clans. The meaning behind the words is, "though you can kill a seasoned warrior, how can you bear to kill an untried youth." The following verse from the "Autumn Song For Work in the Mountains" (Miyagi) is addressed to a fox and plays with the word *kon* (the fox's bark), associating it with *konu* ("I won't come! He/She/It won't come!")

ki ni naru ki ni naru	You trouble me! You trouble me,
oyama no kitsune	mountain fox!
kore hodo matsu no ni	I've waited till now;
naze kon to naru	why do you bark "won't come!"

Since in Chinese and Japanese mythology the fox often assumes the shape of a beautiful woman, the same verse can mean

You trouble me! You trouble me,
bewitching girl of the mountain!
I've waited till now,
so why have you decided you won't come?

*Recorded on Nippon Columbia, AL 132, Side 1.

And, because the fox represents Inari, the God of Harvests, the verse can also mean

> You trouble me! You trouble me,
> fox god of the sacred mountain!
> Why, though I have waited till now,
> do you cry "I won't come!"

A passage from the "Shimoda Song" contains plays on the word *se*, which in this instance means "shoal" and is part of a stative verb as well: *yaruseganai/yarusenai* (to be helpless, to be at a loss, to be heartbroken).

Shimoda no oki ni	Off Shimoda
se ga yottsu	there are four shoals:
omoikiru se ni	the "must give up loving you" shoal,
kiranu se ni	the "won't give up loving you" shoal
toru se ni yarusega-	the "taking" shoal, the "giving" shoal—
nai wai na	I give up! You give up!

"Shimoda Song" (Shizuoka)

Another example of wordplay can be found in the "Song from Tsugaru for Work in the Mountains" where the words "*jūgo ya*" can mean "O Woodcutter!" or can refer both to the fifteenth night in August and the harvest moon. As the song continues, the meaning becomes clear:

jūgo ya shichi wa	fifteen or seventeen years old,
jūgo ni naru kara	after you turn fifteen,
yama nobori	you climb the mountain . . .

"Song from Tsugaru for Work in the Mountains" (Aomori)

In playing on words, Japanese poets often make use of homonyms—words that sound the same but have different meanings. For example, several verses in the "Song On Three

Levels" (Niigata) play with the sound *ai*, which can mean an indigo plant, between, or love.

Chinese poets delight in naming colors—"rich crimson, tender green," "the sun appears, a dot of red," and "a small white cabbage yellowing in the earth" are typical stock lines in Chinese folk literature. However, the Japanese poet feels that to name a thing is to evoke its color: a pinetree implies green and black; an iris, purple or blue; maple leaves, scarlet.

Asama Negoshi no	In the burnt fields
yakeno no naka de	of Negoshi, Asama,
ayame saku to wa	the blooming of iris
shiorashiya	is so lovely!

"Packhorseman's Song from Komoro" (Nagano)

On the other hand, the Japanese folk poet is excited by sound—the cry of the deer, the roar of the waves, rustling noises in the mountains.

mine no arashi ka	A storm in the mountains?
soyo matsukaze ka	The soft wind in the pines?
kitsune no ho koe ka	A fox's barking voice?
yobu koe ka	A calling voice?

"Tree-pruning Song" (Yamagata)

Since the human voice has the flexibility of a musical instrument, Japanese folk-song poets also use onomatopoeia (words that imitate the sound associated with a particular action or object—animate or inanimate—and words whose sounds suggest their meaning) in their lyrics, as well as other ways of playing on sound, independently or together.

Asama-yama-san
naze yake-shansu

Mount Asama!
Why are you burning with envy?

"*Packhorseman's Song from Oiwake*" *(Nagano)*
"*Packhorseman's Song from Komoro*" *(Nagano)*
"*Shinano Oiwake*" *(Nagano)*

nishi-higashi
Matsushima Toshima
me no shita ni

To the west, to the east,
Matsushima, Toshima—
right below your eyes!

"*Saitara's Song*" *(Miyagi)*

tsuite otetsudai
suru ki de kita ka

Did you come to help
with the hulling

"*Sōma Barley-hulling Song*" *(Fukushima)*

orai no mono to
ugai no mono to
nobari de sake nomi ni
sake no sakana ni
nasubi-hi dasari de
shoppegata na ya doyagu

We all
and you all
were invited out for a drink.
For hors d'oeuvres, they
brought out pickled eggplant—
was it salty, buddy!

'*Akita Ondo*" *(Akita)*

By singing the above verse in a heavy Akita accent, the performer emphasizes the sound play, usually to the delight of the audience:

orai no mono do
ugai no mono do
nobari di sagi nomi ni
sage no sagana ni
nasubi-hi dasari di
shoppegata na ya doyagu

"*Akita Ondo*" *(Akita)*

38   *Folk-Song Poetry*

suzume wa **chunchun**	Sparrows go "chunchun!"
karasu ga **kaakaa**	Crows "Caw, caw!"
tombi wa **piihyororo**	Kites "Piihyororo!"
kayaba no naka de	Among the reeds,
saezuru toriko	the crying birdies
gege-jigojigo-peppe	"Gege-jigojigo-peppe!"

"Akita Ondo" (Akita)

The Japanese folk-song poet not only plays with onomatopoeia, as in the preceding verse, but uses it to heighten the lyric's grace, elegance, or pathos.

yurari-yurari to	Wavering,
yosete wa kaesu	it moves to and fro;
nami no se ni noru	it floats on the current of the waves:
aki no tsuki	the autumn moon.

"The Beach Song" (Ibaraki)

Yurari-yurari is onomatopoeia for waving or floating to and fro.

| horo to naita wa | Will I ever forget? |
| wasuraryo ka | how we tried not to cry |

"Packhorseman's Song from Oiwake" (Nagano)

Horo or *horohoro* is onomatopoeia for a situation in which somebody's tears fall in big drops, though he is trying hard not to cry.

Song-titles are particularly significant in Japanese folk music. A title is an indication of a song's genre, its style, its place of origin, its composer, or its content. In addition, a folk song's title frequently alerts the listeners to what the song's composers regard as its most striking formal feature. The title "The Sōma Refrain," for example, indicates that there is a special way in which the people from Sōma put a type of poetic refrain to music. "A Song on Three Levels," the title of a Niigata dance song for O-Bon, the Buddhist Festival for Souls, refers to elements in that song's musical and poetic forms alike—a line of verse repeated three times, and the division of each half of the song into three melodic phrases. Furthermore, the verses of "A Song on Three Levels" are concerned with worlds or levels of experience that are divided into units of three: the past, present, and future; the world of all the Buddhas in the Universe, the world of all living beings, and the world of the self; and the world of art and romance, the world of religion, and the criminal underworld.

Song titles, because of their special function, also serve to emphasize the characteristic interdependence in Japan of music and poetry.

Chapter Four
Types of Japanese Folk Songs

WHEN THE JAPANESE SING their finest songs to strangers, it is a sign of hospitality and trust. For centuries, professional entertainers, among whose recent descendants are the geisha, have popularized the folk songs of their home provinces, towns, villages, or islands by singing them to visitors. And they have flattered and charmed people from other parts of their country by learning and singing their local songs.

Performed outside its home region, a Japanese folk song is no longer limited to its original function. A coal-miner's song, a lullaby, or a festival song can become a banquet-and-party song (*zashiki-uta* or *o-zashiki-uta*), when sung away from home.

A party song (*o-zashiki-uta*) generally refers to any traditional Japanese folk or popular song that is performed by geisha, other professional entertainers, and guests at a sit-down party with music and dancing, eating and drinking. The *o-zashiki* is the room where people wine, dine, and entertain their guests. Many folk songs are known throughout Japan only in their banquet-and-party versions. And there are large numbers of folk songs, such as the "Shimoda Song" (Shizuoka), that have always been party songs.

A party song is designed both to display an entertainer's ability and to make the guests feel like accomplished—if not always refined—connoisseurs of life.

The difference between performing the same song as, say, a lullaby and as a banquet song is as great as the difference between raising a tree in the yard and a miniature tree, a bonsai, in a pot. In its banquet version, the basic structure of the original song is preserved—just as a bonsai remains structurally a complete tree—but is differently perceived, with some of its emotions being submerged, others heightened. For example, in cases where the original song was sung without instrumental accompaniment, the banquet version adds instruments, thus offering the singer new tone colors, new approaches to the melody, and new melodic and rhythmical counterpoints with which to work.

In its setting as a banquet song, the emotional scope of a song's text is often carried way beyond its original limitations. A desperate lullaby by an isolated nursemaid in a backcountry village, far from her own home and family, always underfed and harassed, barely more than a child herself, suddenly serves to describe a whole group of young women in a city entertainment district. The nursemaid's song may be sung by a geisha as a complaint against her employer, as a lament for a personal sadness, or to win a patron.

odoma kwanjin kwanjin an shtotachi'a yokashi yokashi'a yoka obi yoka kimon	We're the beggars, the beggars! they're the nice people. Nice people are fine sashes, fine clothes.
odon ga utchinneba michibachi'a ikero tōru shitogochi hana agyū	If I should drop dead, bury me by the roadside! I'll give a flower to everyone who passes.
hana wa nan no hana tsun-tsun-tsubaki mizu wa ten kara morai-mizu	What kind of flower? the cam-cam-camellia watered by Heaven: alms-water.

"*The Nursemaid's Song from Itsuki Village*" (Kumamoto)

As another example, a remark about local weather and travel conditions in the festival dance song, "A Song on Three Levels," becomes, in the banquet performance of the same song, a sketch of a woman hesitating to become involved in a love affair.

Kashiwazaki kara	From Kashiwazaki
Shiiya made	to Shiiya:
ai ni	between,
Arahama Arasuna	wild seashore (Arahama),
	desolate sands (Arasuna),
Akuta no watashi ga	the ferry at Akuta—
nakayokaro	if there's none, it's just as well.
nakayokaro	If there's none, it's just as well.
ai ni	In love:
arahama arasuna	wild seashore, desolate sands,
akuta no watashi ga	rubbish delivery—
nakayokaro	if there's none, it's just as well.

"A Song on Three Levels" (Niigata)

When performed out of doors on a summer night at the Festival for Souls, the "Song on Three Levels" is a communal song. A dialogue between soloist and chorus, it is accompanied by a drum, with hundreds of people singing, dancing and wandering around. But, when accompanied by the shamisen and performed indoors at any time of year, in front of a smaller number of people (noisy or not), by a solo singer who makes everyone believe the song is addressed to one special person, the "Song on Three Levels" becomes an intimate party song.

In spite of their travels and alterations, folk songs retain a local flavor, much as regional seafood dishes do. The melodies from some areas rush up or down in highly ornamented and carefully controlled bursts of energy, while those of neighboring districts move at a gentler, more measured pace. Songs from the Tsugaru region in Aomori are spectacular virtuoso pieces for singer and instrumentalists alike. Songs from the Shimokita Peninsula in the same prefecture are generally lighter and often contain long passages in *Sprechgesang* (spoken song), to use a contemporary Western term. (The Japanese term for "spoken song" is *hayashi-kotoba*—music-words. *Hayashi-kotoba* are an important part of Japanese folk-song acompaniment and are discussed at greater length in chapter five.

A geisha from a small town or village who achieves fame as an artist, rather than forgetting the festival and work songs of her birthplace, tends to make them an integral part of her repertory. Of course, she may make changes in the music to suit her own preferences and those of her audiences. That is how the prefecture of Ibaraki became famous for a group of lovely folk songs influenced by geisha vocal and instrumental styles. Among these songs are the "Beach Song" (based on an old boatman's song), the "City Ditty from Hitachi," and the "Song in the Ni-agari Tuning from Mito."

Geisha and other folk-song artists act not only as links between the songs as performed in their provincial surroundings and versions performed elsewhere, but also as liaisons between folk song and other vocal and instrumental genres, such as the old popular "city ditty" *(dodoitsu)*, the "snatch of song" (ha-uta), Buddhist hymns, music for the theater, and epic song styles. In fact, some kinds of folk songs are actually based on traditional, urban, popular-song genres. Among the most well-known examples of such adaptations are the *ko-uta* and the *dodoitsu*.

The *ko-uta* (a little song, an air) is a short popular-song style which dates back to the Muromachi Era (ca. 1392–ca. 1573) and is still current. The *ko-uta* singer accompanies himself or herself on the shamisen. The folk-song *ko-uta* is comparatively new and has been somewhat influenced by Western music. Traditional *ko-uta* are through-composed; a folk *ko-uta* is stanzaic. Older *ko-uta* have no refrains, but folk *ko-uta* sometimes do have them.

The traditional *dodoitsu* (city ditty) is a very short, through-composed, erotic songpoem. It is either accompanied by shamisen or read aloud from a collection. (The poem is sung, not intoned, but the singer is, in effect, reading it.) The traditional shamisen accompaniment for a *dodoitsu* is minimal—a subtly-spaced following of the singer's melody; the rhythm is so unobtrusive that at times only a trained ear knows of its existence. The folk city ditty, on the other hand, can be stanzaic. Its shamisen accompaniment is often ostinato, with the same rhythmic and melodic phrase repeated over and over under the singer.

The folk *dodoitsu*'s chief link with the traditional *dodoitsu* is its use of (and variations on) the standard *dodoitsu* melody. However, as in the "City Ditty from Nambu" (Shimokita

Peninsula in Aomori), the folk version may depart almost completely from melodic patterns characteristic of the traditional *dodoitsu*. This is partly because the patterns have been fragmented, and partly because the ostinato accompaniment can distract the listener, at least temporarily. Even those folk *dodoitsu* that remain musically closer to the traditional city ditty are sometimes changed by incorporating other folk songs or folksong styles. The "City Ditty from Hitachi" (Ibaraki), for example, weaves in a packhorseman's song.*

In its turn, folk song has influenced a variety of popular-song genres, ranging from the older *ha-uta* to the modern *enka*.

The *ha-uta* (bits or scraps of song, a snatch of song) are longer popular songs that were performed by professional entertainers of the geisha type during the late Tokugawa Era. *Ha-uta* are still performed, with the shamisen, the bamboo flute *(fue)*, and a variety of percussion instruments as the accompaniment. *Ha-uta* can be stanzaic or through-composed, the *ha-uta*'s poetic form differing with each piece. They often refer to or quote from other musical-poetic repertoires. In one example, the *ha-uta* "Beach-Song Breakup" ("Iso-bushi kuzushi") refers to the folk "Beach Song." In another example, the *ha-uta* "Six-Sections Break-up" ("Rokudan kuzushi") takes "Rokudan" ("Piece in Six Sections"), a theme and variations for *koto* (zither), as its point of departure. *Ha-uta* lyrics are typically allusive as well. For a knowledgeable audience, the *ha-uta*'s subtle references to other music and poetry provide an opportunity for an impressive display of an artist's virtuosity. Such references may be to melodies; to song texts; to a piece's form, for example, through capsulization, as in a *kuzushi* (break-up); to a piece's characteristic rhythm, and so on.

The *kuzushi* is an important category within the *ha-uta*. To make a *kuzushi*, the composer reshapes either the accompaniment or the vocal part, or both. In the "Oiwake kuzushi" of Hokkaidō, for instance, the first two long melodic phrases of the "Packhorseman's Art Song from Esashi" are compressed into a little stanza and combined musically with another party-folk piece, the "Song of the Pretty Girls" (Ōshima in Tōkyō Municipality).

Enka are the aggressive outcries of lonely vagabonds and

---

*As performed by Fukuda Yōko (Tōshiba LP TR-6014, Side 1, Item #9).

desperados. They are hybrids of folk song, popular song, and military or dance band music. As such, *enka* are accompanied by both an orchestra or band and by Japanese instruments—the shamisen, the *kokyū* (its name means Chinese violin), and, most often, the *shakuhachi*.

The *shakuhachi* is made from pieces of hollowed-out bamboo. It sounds like a flute, but its shape is more like that of other woodwinds; like a clarinet, it flares out slightly at the bottom. The *shakuhachi* has a violent history behind it that makes it a very appropriate accompaniment for *enka*. The original instrument was made from a single piece of bamboo which the musician could use as a weapon. Many of the first *shakuhachi* players were swordsmen-spies who traveled around the country disguised as mendicant Buddhist monks. Since a monk is supposed to be unarmed, the musical instrument made a good cover.

The postwar *enka* singer's voice is sharp, rather twangy and harsh; the singer ends each stanza with a characteristic quavering note. But an *enka* singer's voice can also be gentle, sweet, and melancholy, as *enka* were sung in the twenties and thirties, and again in the 1970s. Both men and women sing enka. When women sing them, they dress in bright-colored, glittering, traditional men's costumes. (It is common practice in many of the performing arts in Japan for women to wear men's costumes and to sing, dance, or act in masculine genres, roles, and voices.)

O-Bon is the summer festival for the souls of one's dead friends and relatives. It takes place sometime between the middle of July and before the twentieth of August, the time varying from place to place depending on whether or not the old calendar is followed. The festival, which lasts for four days, was originally centered around the fifteenth night of the seventh lunar month. It comes right after another important summer festival, Tanabata, the star festival. During O-Bon, the souls are visited at their graves in a ceremony called *o-haka-mairi* (pilgrimage to the honored graves). The souls are also welcomed back with special lanterns to visit the living—which is why many Westerners know O-Bon as the Festival of Lanterns—and guided to their families' homes with small welcoming fires *(o-mukae)*.

People who have died within the year are given a special religious service called the *nyū-Bon* (entering Bon) or *nii-Bon* (new Bon). A Buddhist priest comes to the home of the head of the family and chants prayers for the dead at the family altar. Then there is a feast for relatives and close friends, each of whom is given a box of special sweet cakes.

During O-Bon, or Festival for Souls, the living regale the souls of friends and relatives with songs and dances. The Bon Festival Dance, which is the climax of the four-day festival, involves the whole community. It is also a major occasion for individual performers to show off their skills as dancers, singers, poets, or musicians.

Many narrative songs performed at the Bon Festival Dance deal with secular events such as battles, love affairs, and gamblers' wars. A substantial number of these narrative songs have to do with death by violence. Such stories are appropriate to summer, which in Japan is the season of ghosts and restless souls. But even when songs make no direct reference to the festival itself, a religious feeling pervades them.

Bon festival musicians and singers often perform on a small, high, square stage, which is sometimes on wheels, or on top of a *yagura,* a three-story wooden platform rather like a tower. Below the musicians, old people, young people, and children dance in circles around the tower, like ripples around a large rock.

Young men in kimonos or blue jeans half dance and half swagger, roaring the vocal accompaniments. Middle-aged ladies in kimonos dance with self-conscious grace. The singers looking down on the swaying crowd sing the same song in relays for four, five, and six hours, sometimes even longer, each one doing the melody and shouts of encouragement in his or her own personal style, with the other singers yelling vocal accompaniments in the soloist's ear. The drummer's arms, hands, and sticks dance in the air between drumbeats. The flutist switches flutes to match each singer. (The flutes are different sizes and, therefore, in different keys.) It is indeed a performance enjoyed by musicians and dancers alike.

Whether or not there is a tower or stage to dance around, many Bon dances are still circle-dances. But there are also numerous communities where everybody, including the musicians, dances down the main thoroughfare in a long parade. In earlier times, people all over Japan danced from evening till dawn. Now, in many of the bigger towns, Bon dances last only until midnight, although there are some towns where the dancing goes on continuously for four days and nights. The music is intoxicating, at once expressing sorrow and relieving it, turning it to rapture. Bon songs are full of reassurances for the living and dead alike: there will be a splendid harvest this year; our town is still on the map and still famous for its scenery, its wares, its songs; the girls are still sexy; life is still going on; we are all right; we have missed you. Songs that entertain and eulogize souls are also fitting for O-Bon. The "Ballad from Aikawa" (Sado Island in Niigata) relates episodes from the *Gempei gundan, Tales of the Taira and Minamoto Armies.* The "Song from Yagi" (Gumma and Tochigi) is the setting for a tale of lovers who committed double suicide. Another story told to the "Song from Yagi" is of chivalrous desperados the likes of Kunisada Chūji, the gambling boss from the village of Kunisada in the Sawa District of Kózuke Province (now Gumma Prefecture). Yet a third "Song from Yagi" story tells about Sakura Sōgoro, the courageous headman of Yoakashi Village in the province of Shimōsa (now Chiba and Ibaraki). Sōgoro was crucified with his innocent family in 1645, because he presented a petition to the central government against his overlord's devastating taxations of the villages. (He was not a Christian—a form of crucifixion was one of the capital punishments during the Tokugawa Period.)

Among the many important varieties of Bon-dance songs are the *jinku,* the *okesa,* and the *owara.*

The *jinku* (dreadful verse) is now also sung as a party song. *Jinku* melodies are extremely graceful. Some are comparatively simple, like that of the "Ajigasa jinku" (Aomori) and the "Niitsu jinku" (Niigata). Others are more elaborate, like that of the "Akita jinku" (Akita). The verses of *jinku* are light but elegant.

Okesa are half Bon-dance and half party songs. They are primarily associated with Niigata Prefecture, especially with Sado Island, home of the *okesa*'s geisha inventor. (There are a number of charming legends about the origins of the *okesa,* but the story of a geisha composer appears to be the most feasible.

The same *okesa* may be sung pensively in a slow tempo, or quite fast. Whatever its tempo, the *okesa* is always performed with snap and passion. *Okesa* are always accompanied by shamisen, and almost always by bamboo flute *(fue),* drums, and voice. Some of the greatest *okesa* singers have been men; the twentieth-century singer Murata Bunzō, from Sado Island, is just one example. There are famous *owara* songs or *ohara* songs throughout Japan, from the "Ohara Song from Kagoshima" in the south, to the northeastern "Owara Song from Tsugaru" (Aomori). The interjection *owara* or *ohara* appears in the text or the refrain of these songs, although no one is clear on what *owara* means. Some *owara* songs are fast and energetic; others are slow and graceful. Unlike the *jinku,* whose verse form is constant all over Japan, the verse form of an *owara* song varies from place to place. Introductory and closing remarks in song are typical of some *owara*. And several *owara* are designed so that the composer and poet can insert a passage from another kind of song.

Instrumental accompaniment varies from Bon song to Bon song. For the "Sōma Bon Song" (Fukushima), the instrumental accompaniment is a flute *(fue)* and large drum. In the "Song from Yagi" (Gumma and Tochigi) there is a flute, hand-gong *(kane),* two pairs of large hourglass-shaped drums *(tsuzumi),* and a large sake cask played with thick drumsticks. The "Ballad from Aikawa" (Sado Island in Niigata) is accompanied by shamisen and one or two drums, and sometimes, a flute as well. Many very old Bon songs, including the "Dance from Matsuyama" (Okayama) and the "Bon Song of Tsukudajima" (Tōkyō) are accompanied only by clapping unless somebody plays a flute with the refrains or a drum with the vocal accompaniments.

In Japan, October and November are the traditional months for weddings. These are the months of the least heavy farm work, the months before heavy snows blanket half the country. Trousseau-carrying songs, the *naga-mochi-uta* (songs for the long carrying), refer to the bygone custom of carrying the bride's trousseau to her new home, often over long distances. Since *naga-mochi* also means lasting or enduring, it is an auspicious title for a wedding song. As far away as America, at a June catered affair, a Japanese bride and groom may still request the performance of a *naga-mochi-uta*. Even accompanied by a jazz piano, with the gloriously long-held notes considerably shortened, the song remains quite powerful.

Nowadays, trousseau-carrying songs are played on radio and television from October through December (including Japanese-language radio and television outside Japan.) But *naga-mochi-uta* are not only presented on folk-music programs; they are also played as background music to advertise resorts, hotels, and wedding palaces for the catered affair and the honeymoon. The carrying of a bride's trousseau across an autumn or winter landscape is a poignant scene, even in the most violent sword-fighting movie, and adroit business and public relations people are quick to take advantage of the nostalgia aroused by a *naga-mochi-uta*.

The verses of trousseau-carrying songs picture the joy and beauty of a wedding as well as the sadness of the bride's leaving her family and home. The following verses come from a trousseau-carrying song from Miyagi.

chō yo hana yo to
sodateta musume
kyō wa tanin no
te ni wataru

Our daughter, raised
like a butterfly! a flower!
today passes
into other hands.

kyō wa hi mo yoshi
tenki mo yoi shi
musubi awasete
en to naru

This is an auspicious day,
and the weather is beautiful!
A couple is united;
a karma is fulfilled.

kokyō koishi to
omou na musume
kokyō tōza no
kari no yado

Daughter, don't think,
"I miss my old home!"
Your old home was but
a momentary shelter.

medeta medeta no
kasanaru toki wa
Ama-no-Iwado mo
oshi-hiraku

At such a happy,
happy moment,
they fling open the very door
of the Heavenly Cave!

(This is that same cave in which the Sun Goddess Amaterasu had hidden herself.)

saasa otachi da
o-nagori-oshiya
kondo kuru toki'a
mago tsurete

Well, well, she's leaving.
How sad it is to part!
The next time she comes,
bringing a grandchild.

Trousseau-carrying Song (Miyagi)

Wedding songs come under the general heading of congratulations songs *(iwai-uta* or *o-iwai-uta)*, which are also sung at housewarmings and on New Year's Day. Many congratulation songs are slow and highly ornamented. The beautiful and touching words often refer to the tortoise and the crane, symbols of longevity and married love, and to the pine, symbol of fidelity and youthful energy. Wedding and New Year songs are full of late autumn and winter radiance.

In the 1980s, these songs were still being sung by both professionals and amateurs at festive occasions, and in folk-song bars and folk-song competitions.

Songs that were once work songs are now also sung as banquet-and-party songs and form another major part of the Japanese folk repertory. Many of these may originally have been songs about work that were performed at religious and secular festivals rather than songs sung by people actually at work.*)

Work songs have been used as dance music by geisha and dancers connected with every type of theater from the Kabuki to the equivalent of the Radio City Music Hall. In addition to work songs that have become party songs, many songs based on work-song styles and subjects have been composed specifically for theatrical and private party entertainment.

What follows is only a partial list of Japanese work songs, but these have all been frequently recorded.

shiro-kaki-uta	rice field plowing and hoeing songs
nae-tori-uta	seedling-taking songs (sung when taking seedlings from a rice-nursery bed and preparing to transplant them)
ta-ue-uta	rice-planting songs (sung while transplanting the seedlings in the paddy field)

---

*Professor Matsumoto Keishin of Sōma is of this opinion.

ta no kusa-tori-uta	rice field weeding songs (sung while weeding grass in the rice fields, to keep out snakes and hungry cows and let the rice grow without being overwhelmed by the grass)
kusa-kari-uta	mowing and grass-cutting songs
mugi-maki-uta	barley-sowing and millet-sowing songs
kome-tsuki-uta	
momi-suri-uta *momi-zuri-uta*	rice-hulling songs
hie-tsuki-uta	millet-pounding songs
mugi-uchi-uta	barley-threshing songs
kome-togi-uta	rice-washing songs
tawara-tsumi-uta	bag-loading songs (The bags are made of straw and carry everything from rice to charcoal.)
mochi-tsuki-uta	ricecake-making songs (The cakes are made by pounding steamed rice.)
mame-hiki-uta *mame-suri-uta*	bean-grinding songs
ina-koki-uta	threshing songs
usu-hiki-uta	milling or miller's songs
ko-hiki-uta	flour-grinding songs
cha-tsumi-uta	tea-picking songs
cha-momi-uta	tea-rubbing songs
ushi-oi-uta *ushi-kata-bushi*	cowherd's songs
ko-mori-uta	lullabies, songs for minding the children, and nursemaids' songs

hagi-kari-uta	bush-clover-cutting songs (Bush clover is used in fodder for cattle or horses.)
shiba-kari-uta	brushwood-gathering songs and firewood-cutting songs
kinoko-tori-uta	mushroom-picking songs
yama-uta	mountain songs or hillside songs (sung while at work in the mountains or hills, either cutting wood or gathering grasses and plants for feeding horses and cattle, putting in soup, or eating with rice)
kobiki-uta	sawyer's songs and lumber-hauling songs
ki-nagashi-uta	log-driving songs
ikada-nagashi-uta	raftsmen's songs (Ten or so logs are bound together to make a raft; then the rafts are fastened to each other in a long line, and the men pole them downriver.)
kikori-uta	woodcutter's songs
kiyari-bushi *kiyari-uta*	chants sung while carrying heavy lumber or the like; also used as congratulation songs
kiyari ondo *do-tsuki-uta* *ji-tsuki-uta*	earth-tamping songs*
tatara-uta *fui-go-uta*	bellows and iron-ore bellows songs (The bellows are worked with the feet.)
zeni-fuki-uta	coiner's and minting songs (An eighteenth-century minting song from Miyagi is supposed to be the song from which Saitarō, a foundryman turned fisherman, created "Saitara's Song," a rowing-cum-festival song.)
kanayama-uta	miner's songs (gold mines, iron mines, etc.)

*See Embree, John F., *Japanese Peasant Songs,* pages 54–65. Philadelphia: American Folklore Society, 1944.

Japanese Folk Songs 53

tankō-bushi	coal-miner's songs
ishi-kiri-uta	stone-cutter's and quarrying songs
sakaya-uta *sake-zukuri-uta*	sake-makers songs and brewer's songs
(sakaya) nagashi-uta	brewery washing-away and washing-off songs (These songs are sung while workers prepare to brew rice wine [sake] during the annual November washing of the brewery implements.)
moto-suri-uta	rice-malt-grinding songs (another brewery song)
tabako-maki-uta	tobacco-rolling songs
kuwa-tsumi-uta	mulberry-picking songs (Mulberries are fed to the silkworms.)
koya-uta	dyer's songs
ito-kuri-uta	spinning songs
hata-ori-uta	weaver's songs
seishi-uta *kami-suki-uta*	paper-making songs
urushi-kaki-uta	lacquer-mixing, lacquer-extracting, and lacquer-making songs
-uri-uta	vendor's songs
tsuna-hiki-uta	rope-hauling and line-hauling songs
ami-hiki-uta	fishnet-hauling songs
ami-noshi-uta	fishnet-spreading songs
tairyō-bushi	songs celebrating or hoping for a fine catch of fish
funa-kogi uta *ro-kogi-uta*	sculling songs
funa-uta *funa-kata-uta*	boat and boatmen's songs

One of the best examples of the interrelationship between work songs and party songs in Japan is to be found in that between packhorsemen's songs and the *oiwake,* referred to earlier as the packhorseman's art song.

Packhorsemen's songs *(mago-uta* or *uma-kata-bushi)* were sung in times past by men who led horses, carrying travelers and their luggage, over mountain roads. It was a dull, tiring job, and the leader's loneliness and boredom found expression in verse.

nagai dōchū de	On your long journey,
ame furu naraba	when it rains,
washi no namida to	please, remember
omoute kure	my tears!
ao yo naku na you	Blacky! don't cry, horse!
ora uchi'a chikai	We're almost home.
mori no naka kara	You can see the lights
hi ga mieru	from inside the woods.
kokoro-sabishiya	Ah, how lonely it is!
bakuro no yomichi	a wretched packhorse-drover's night road,
naru wa kutsuwa no	the jangling of the bit
oto bakari	the only sound.

Verses common to many packhorsemen's songs

Now the packhorsemen's songs are virtuoso pieces accompanied by bells *(suzu)* that jingle like bridlebells or sleighbells, or the *ekiro,* a bell that was hung on post-horses. Other accompaniments include the shouting voice and the *shakuhachi,* which, with its range of at least three octaves and its variety of tone qualities, sounds like a flute's soul. Occasionally a shamisen and drum *(taiko)* are added to the *mago-uta* accompaniment.

Oiwake or *oiwake-bushi* are professional folk-singers' musical and poetic versions of the packhorsemen's songs. The *oiwake* dates back to the late Tokugawa Period. This genre is named after Oiwake, an old post town in what is now Nagano Prefecture. Oiwake was famous for its fine packhorsemen's songs and its entertainment district.

While the melodies of most of the original packhorsemen's songs appear to vary little from place to place, the *oiwake* has developed into widely differing tunes. The *oiwake* has also incorporated at least one other work-song genre, the boatmen's song *(funa-uta)*.

Oiwake are characterized by the singer's delight in nature in contrast to his terrible loneliness. Although many *oiwake* verses are explosively emotional, the singer often reveals the pathos of his heartache by singing of the beauty of iris in a field, the cries of plovers in the deep night, mist on a beach, the charm of a plateau, the "autumn brocade" of leaves.

Oiwake are accompanied by *shakuhachi*, shamisen, or both. Many *oiwake* also call for shouting voice. Occasionally a *koto* (zither) or a drum is also included.

Oiwake are sung by both men and women. For one or two there are men's versions and women's versions, but, except for the fact that the women sing in higher keys, there don't appear to be any real differences.

In this century, both the *oiwake* and the packhorsemen's songs have become singing competition pieces. One *oiwake*, the "Esashi oiwake" (Hokkaidō), previously referred to as "The Packhorseman's Art Song from Esashi," has become as great a challenge to Japanese folksingers as "Porgi, Amor" is to sopranos who want to sing Mozart opera. Several Japanese record companies have issued long-playing record albums consisting entirely of performances of "Esashi oiwake."

"Esashi oiwake" is composed of four parts:

1) the *mae-uta*, the before-song or preceding song.
2) an *ai-no-te*, an instrumental interlude. Whether or not "Esashi oiwake" is performed with shamisen or percussion, this section changes tempo and rhythm. It becomes faster, and the beat is more obvious.
3) the *hon-uta*, the main song or original song. This section most resembles the original packhorseman's song, on which "Esashi oiwake" is based.
4) the *ato-uta*, the after-song. In effect, this section is a musical and poetic coda.

Many complete texts have been printed for "Esashi oiwake," but *mae-uta*, *hon-uta*, and *ato-uta* texts are often regarded as separate entities. A particular *mae-uta* text need not always be followed by a particular *hon-uta* text; a particular *hon-uta* text need not always be followed by the same *ato-uta* text.

56 *Japanese Folk Songs*

    Because of their dignity and emotional force, a number of texts have been set to "Esashi oiwake" melodies, which glorify the martial, patriotic spirit. The text below, with its references to General Nogi Maresuke and to victories over the Russians on Chinese territory, dates from the 1904–1905 Russo-Japanese War.

ani wa Nanzan	My elder brother at Nanshan,
otōto wa Ryojun	my younger brother at Lüshun—
isamashiya	how valiant they were!
chirite kanbashi	Falling, they are Nogi's
Nogi no hana	fragrant blossoms.
chichi mo kokka no	My father, too,
mata chūseki yo	was a pillar of the nation!
shi-shite gokoku no	In death, he becomes our country's
kami to naru	guardian god.
noboru asahi wa	There is a single rising sun
sekai ni hitotsu	in the world.
Nogi no homare mo	Nogi's glory, too,
mata hitotsu	is unique.
hito wa ichidai	"Man has one life;
na wa matsudai yo	fame is eternal!
tora sae shi-shite	E'en the tiger, though he dies,
kawa nokosu	leaves his skin behind."

"Esashi oiwake" (Hokkaidō)

    However, the most moving "Esashi oiwake" texts are those which describe the beauties of Hokkaidō, the loneliness of a sailors's life, the longing for love. (Ex. 1.)

Matsumae Esashi no	In Matsumae, Esashi,
Tsubana no Hama de	the red-light district of Tsubana,
yansa no e	
suita dōshi no	at the "Beach Shack," lovers'
naki-wakare	tearful parting
tsurete yuku ki wa	Oh, how he longs
yama-yama naredo	to take her with him! but
onna tōsanu	there are places
basho ga aru	where a woman's not allowed.

shimo to yuki to ni shiore wa suredo watashi 'a Ezo-matsu iro kaenu	"Though others may fade in frost and snow, I am a silver fir; my color will not change." (Though other lovers may droop in adversity, I am a silver fir of Ezo, the Barbarian Isle: my love will never fade.)
nami ni senri no omoi o nosete tsuki ni saosasu ikada-bune	Over the waves, a raft burdened with a thousand miles of thoughts is drawn by the moon...

"*Esashi oiwake*" *(Hokkaidō)*

Although some categories of Japanese folk song include only small numbers of songs, they are generally regarded as significant.

Obako (the belle) are lyrical dance songs from Akita and Yamagata Prefectures that celebrate the local, beautiful girls. Like Soochow in China, Akita and Yamagata have been famous for centuries for their attractive and brilliant women. Akita was the birthplace of the Heian-Period poetess Ono-no-Komachi.

The *kudoki* or *kudoki-bushi* (persuading songs) are long but light songs, whose stanzas describe the scenic beauties of a particular region. The *kudoki* may also tell a story.

The *ondo* is a ballad and/or a dance song. It always involves a lead singer, the *ondo-tori* (*ondo*-maker), and a singing or shouting chorus. Ondo range in feeling and language from light songs to elevated, emotional, and heroic songs like "Aikawa ondo" ("Ballad from Aikawa"), to mixtures of the murderous and comical like "Kawachi ondo" ("Ballad from Kawachi") and "Gōshū ondo" ("Ballad from Ōmi"). The "Akita ondo" is a dancing *ondo*. So is the "New 'Tōkyō ondo,'" a modern folk

Ex. 1.   "*Esashi oiwake*" Vocal Score

wa — ya- ma-
ya- ma —
na- re- do — ne — SOI! o-n- na —
— tô
sa- nu — ba-sho —
ga — a- ru
Kakegoe cue: A SOI, SOI—SOI!
HON-UTA
shi-mo — to —
— SOI! yu-ki —

to ni
soi! shi-o- re wa
soi! su- rē-
do soi, soi!
wa-ta- shi'a
soi!
E-zo- ma tsu
soi!

i- ro Ka-
e- nu
Kakegoe cue: soi, soi!
ATO-UTA
na- mi ni se-n-ri
no o-mo-
i o no- se-
te ne soi! tsu-Ki
ni sa- o-
sa- su
i-Ka- da- bu- ne

song composed by Nakayama Shimpei. "New 'Tōkyō ondo'" was actually a popular song based on a folk song but is now in the process of becoming a folk song.

The Ōtsu picture was a type of folk painting that was very popular during the reign of the Emperor Genroku (1688–1704). Ōtsu pictures were sold near the temple of Miidera, outside the town of Ōtsu in what is now Shiga Prefecture. These paintings depicted favorite folk heroes, and later, the latest love stories. Benkei, the Herculean retainer of the twelfth-century warrior hero Minamoto Yoshitsune, was associated with Miidera, and his is one of the earliest extant Ōtsu pictures. In folk song, *ōtsu-e* or *ōtsu-e-bushi* (Ōtsu picture songs) are narrative songs and, in some places such as Aizu (Fukushima), congratulation songs as well.

Counting songs are found in both child and adult repertoires. The texts play on words with the same sounds as the numbers one through fifteen.

muttsu-a e	**six** —
muri dā oyashu ni	exploited **UN**reasonably
tsukawarete	by all their parents,
to no yubiko kara	blood flows
chi-ko nagasu	from her ten fingers!
kore mo Yasaburo-a e	

"The Yasaburo Song" (Aomori)

yottsu	**four** —
yozake-ko	just can't stop
nakanaka yamenu	**night**time drinking!
bara no naka kara	roses come,
bara-ko deru	roses come
bara-ko deru	from rosebush roots

"The Tanto Song" (Akita)

ichi ni tachibana	One-two, mandarin orange;
ni ni kakitsubata	Two, too, iris;
san ni **sa**gari-fuji	Three, drooping wistaria;
shi ni **shishi**-botsan	Four, the lion's peony;
tsutsu I-yama no	Five, the thousand cherry trees
sambon-zakura	on Yi Mountain;

Japanese Folk Songs 63

muttsu murasaki	Six, dyed with purple
kikyō ni somete	bell-flowers;
nanatsu Nandemo	Seven, anything;
yatsu yamabuki yo	Eight, yellow rose!
kokonotsu koume wa	Nine, the little plum tree
shiracha ni somete	dyed light brown;
tō de tonosama	Ten; his Lordship's
aoi no gomon	hollyhock crest.

a children's game song (Aichi)

Even an interjection may become the distinguishing characteristic of a Japanese folk song. The *yosare* or *yoshare* song originated in the northeast but has spread north to Hokkaido and also to the south. The interjection *"yoshare,"* which is dialect for *"O-yoshi nasai!"* ("Quit it!"), is part of the song's refrain. In many *yoshare* songs, the interjection has nothing to do with the meaning of the text but is used merely as a formal device to round off the melody or as part of a refrain at the beginning, middle, or end of a musical-poetic section (either stanzaic or through-composed). In such cases, the interjection becomes the name of the song or, as the song spreads and develops into many versions, the name of its type. On the other hand, some interjections used in this way have retained their original meanings. Occasionally the interjection is onomato-poetic, as in "Kotsu-kotsu-bushi" (the Knock-knock Song) of Ōita Prefecture.

Other examples of songs with interjections that are a significant part of the song's structure include the following:

the "Aiya! Song"	
the "Haiya! Song"	(national)
the "Hanya! Song"	
the "Tanto Song"	(Akita and Aomori)
the "It-cha-It-cha Song"	(Tokoyo Municipality and Chiba)
the "Sōran Song"	(Hokkaidō)
"Zarantoshō"	(Miyagi)

"Kanchororin"	(Sōma in Fukushima)
the "Beach Song"	(Ibaraki)
the "Knock-knock! Song"	(Ōita)

The fact that folksingers and their songs move from place to place gives a small repertoire of songs an extended range of poetic and musical possibilities. In one area, for example, there may be several melodies for a single song. The "Refrain" from the city of Sōma in Fukushima has northern and southern neighborhood versions, as does the "Sōma Barley-hulling Song." Or there can be different versions of a song within the same basic musical-poetic form and under the same name. The "Breakdown Song from Tsugaru' and the "Tsugaru Aiya! Song" (both from Aomori) are examples of this, as is the "Thirty-Bushel Cargo Boat Song" from Osaka.

There are songs with the same melody but many different texts. These include story-songs, such as the "Song from Yagi," and lyric songs, such as "Esashi oiwake." Usually, one or two of the texts are widely familiar; the rest are known only by local singers, scholars, and perhaps a few folk-song amateurs outside the area, but can often be found in books or on records.

There are many songs, such as the "Nursemaid's Song from Itsuki Village," that have old and new versions, both of which are still performed although one may be more popular. The difference between these versions may be musical, textual, or a combination of the two. There is also a subdivision of this type, in which the songs have a distinct traditional tune *(seichō)* version. The "Song from Hakata" and the "Traditional-tune 'Song from Hakata'" (Fukuoka) are examples of this subdivision. But when talking about a particular song, even singers themselves tend to call it *hon-mono* (the real thing) or *hontō no* [song title] (the real/proper [song title]) rather than *seichō*.

Some songs are sung together so often as a medley that it becomes difficult to think of them separately. "Saitara's Song" and the "Jinku from Toshima" (Miyagi) are commonly performed as "The Fine Fishing Medley"; another unspecified song may also precede the two.

Frequently singers and composers insert one song or a fragment of a song into another song, to add an extra touch of nostalgia, set a scene, or heighten a mood, drawing striking musical-poetic parallels or contrasts. In the "New 'Bon-Festival Song from Hokkaidō'" the poet-arranger, Fujito Shūjirō, inserted the first two phrases of Esashi oiwake halfway through the stanza of the original festival song. He relied on the emotional implications of the *oiwake*'s melody to add a startling touch of strength, dignity, and profound sadness to that good-natured Bon music. At the same time, the *oiwake* phrases can be sung over the second half of one Bon-song verse and the first half of the following verse, reminding listeners that a typical way to perform "Esashi oiwake" is over an ostinato rhythm.

Many folk songs are also sung by alternating soloists, as in some performances of the "Ballad from Aikawa" (Niigata), the "Barley-and-Such Song" (Toyama), or the "Shimoda Song" (Shizuoka). A song can be performed by soloist and chorus, as in the "Rural 'Song on Three Levels'" (Niigata); by chorus, as in "The Madara Island Song from Nanao (Ishikawa)"; or in relays that go on for hours, even for days and nights, as with Bon Festival songs. There are songs such as "A Song-Quarrel from Ume" (Ōita), in which there can be not only two soloists but two melodies that alternate from verse to verse.

Such a variety of techniques and their widespread use contributes to the vitality of the Japanese folk-song repertory. This repertory thrives on a constant exchange between folk-song and other musical genres, providing composers with material and techniques for new folk songs and assuring the skilled maintenance of old songs.

Chapter Five
Musical Accompaniment

THE ACCOMPANIMENT USED with a Japanese folk song is very important and gives it a distinct personality. Although songs may vary as a result of local, national, rural, or urban influences, the choice of accompaniment can transform a song entirely. The romantic banquet-song from Shizuoka, the "Shimoda Song," for example, becomes aggressively bawdy when accompanied only by clapping hands and shouting voices. But with shamisen and drum, the same song becomes urbane and pensive. Another example is the Hokkaidō folk song, "Esashi oiwake," which is austerely beautiful without accompaniment. When another singer, in the dual role of listener and accompanist, shouts an accompaniment, the feelings expressed in the lyrics are accentuated. Accompanied by percussion, kettle lids, and the like, "Esashi oiwake" is both elegant and homespun, rather as if the singer is being accompanied by horse's hooves. But when accompanied by *shakuhachi* and shouting voice, "Esashi oiwake" gains poignancy and nobility. When shamisen ostinato is added to the *shakuhachi* and shouting voice, however, the nobility is muted and the singer works in relation to a new rhythmic tension. The emotional weight has been shifted again.

Through use of accompaniment, a song may contain contradictory, dualistic, or dialectic qualities, as when a melancholy melody is sung against boisterous strings, winds, and percussion. Duality is evident in the melodies of songs like the "Tsugaru Aiya! Song," or "Mountain-work Song from Tsugaru" (Aomori) and the "Reed-cutting Song" from Miyazaki Prefecture, which are sung in either of two modes, the major or minor mode in Western transcription. In still other songs, such as "The Cowherd's Song from Nambu" (Aomori), the melody is divided between two modes or scales, or moves to and fro between them, as it does in a version of "Come Right In" (Yamagata). In some songs, the singer has a choice of tempi or rhythms. The "Tsugaru Band" (Aomori), for instance, can be sung in a fast triple rhythm (♩ ♪ ♩ ♪) or in a fast duple rhythm (♫ ♫).*

In Japan, there is a close relationship between instrumental and vocal music in that, as in India, the traditional musician is trained from the beginning to "sing" his or her instrument, using specified mnemonics (words or syllables representing the instrument's particular sounds and its playing techniques). These mnemonics differ for each instrument, and sometimes for each instrumental style or school. Mnemonics are also used by folk musicians; in fact, there is at least one category of Japanese folk music that is based on mnemonics entirely—the *baka-bayashi* (idiot's band music), with its singing drums, flute, and gong. Followers of Japanese films may remember Kurosawa Akira's "Donzoko" ("The Lower Depths", in which the last scene was built around *baka-bayashi*. Another example of sung instrumental music is the *saimon,* an old type of Japanese narrative singing in which the singer imitates the twanging of a lute *(biwa)* or shamisen, not only directly by using mnemonics, but indirectly throughout the song when his voice vibrates as if he is plucking his vocal cords. This style of singing continues in the Bon-dance song, "Ballad from Ōmi."

While there are individual pieces and some song genres, such as the lullaby, that have no accompanying voices *(kakegoe* or *hayashi),* vocal accompaniment is one of the prinicpal elements in most Japanese folk songs.

Kakegoe literally means hanging voice(s): the voice or voices that come in at certain points and on which the singer hangs the

---

*Compare the performance of "The Tsugaru Band" by Asari Miki on Nippon Victor 45 rpm (MV–544–S) with that by Sudō Un'ei in *TMDZS,* Side 2, Item #7.

song. At the same time, the voices hang on the song, like tassles on a bridle.

Kakegoe are rhythmic shouts or calls that give singers a chance to catch their breath and encourage them to continue. They are part of a song's formal structure, both as music and as words. A *kakegoe* may work in close relation to either the vocal line or an instrumental accompaniment such as the percussion, or it may interweave with voice and instrument alike. For example, shouts can form part of the drum pattern and, at the same time, act as cues for the singer's voice. In folk song, the various vocal and instrumental lines often create rhythmic and melodic designs like those found in certain Japanese puzzles made from interlocking pieces of wood. A single melodic or rhythmic pattern may also be divided among several instruments and voices.

Kakegoe underscore the end of one melodic phrase and the beginning of another, often weaving phrases together. At times, *kakegoe* point up internal divisions in a song's verse form(s).

Either by reflection or contrast, *kakegoe* accentuate a song's mood. The solo *kakegoe* in "Esashi oiwake" emphasizes the emotional power of the music, the beauty of the words, the nearness to the sea that inspired this song. Here the singer and the *kakegoe* meet each other as the surfer meets the perfect wave; split-second timing is essential. In the "Ballad from Aikawa," the *kakegoe* is simple in that, for one thing, it comes after every two lines of verse and underlines the slow, dignified movement of the story. The two-part *kakegoe* for the "Fine Fishing Medley" of Miyagi Prefecture provides an ostinato that marks the elegance and sensuousness of the melodies and, in the entrances of the second *kakegoe* part, focuses on the ends and beginnings of the melodic phrases. The *kakegoe* for the "Teradomari okesa" from Niigata is as delicate as the melody and the shamisen accompaniment, while that of "The Dance from Awa" (Tokushima) is both a reflection of the jagged percussion, flute, and shamisen accompaniment and a contrast to the melancholy voice.

Japanese folksingers think of every song as having its own particular *kakegoe*, although they know that many songs actually have related or similar *kakegoe*. With few exceptions, Japanese folks-song books include only part of the *kakegoe* for each song (when they are included at all), and usually do not indicate the tone of voice or even the rhythmic pattern. There can often be more than one voice quality for the same *kakegoe,* even when its basic rhythm remains the same. Consequently, *kakegoe* must be learned by ear. *Kakegoe* vary from place to place. Many songs from Sōma have **"ā choi, choi!"** or **"ā kora ya no ya!"** as characteristic *kakegoe,* while songs from Akita often have **"k-taka sassa!" "k'taka korya! korya!"** and similar calls. Regional differences were probably far more pronounced in the past, when communication was limited and always difficult.

Often *kakegoe* provide additional links between songs, as well as a way to hear their differences. "The Fine Fishing Song from Haragama" (Fukushima) and "Saitara's Song" (Miyagi) are related through their refrains and their *kakegoe.* The same *kakegoe* appear at the same places in the two songs—before the last line of a verse and halfway through the refrain. (Ex. 2.)

sorya Sōma oki kara
hashiri-komu fune wa
(kakegoe) **ā korya korya!**
Myōjin-maru yo
refrain:
arya e-e no sorya
(kakegoe) **ā korya korya!**
kyō mo dairyō da *ne*

The boat rushing home
from the sea off Sōma
ā korya korya!
is the Radiant God!

arya e-e no sorya
ā korya korya!
Today, too, is fine fishing!

"Fine Fishing Song from Haragama" (Fukushima)

Matsushima no sayo
Zuiganji hodo no
(kakegoe) **ā korya korya!**
tera mo nai to e
refrain:
arya e-e to sorya
(kakegoe) **ā korya korya!**
dairyo da ne

There is no temple
to equal the Zuiganji
ā korya korya!
on Matsushima.

arya e-e to sorya
ā korya korya!
It's fine fishing!

"Saitara's Song" (Miyagi)

In the "Fine Fishing Song from Haragama," after the refrain there is an additional *kakegoe:* **ha, dairyō, dairyō!"** while "Saitara's Song" is sung over the *kakegoe* ostinato **"en-ya do-tto, en-ya do-tto...."** It is impossible to tell from the words or

Ex. 2. Comparative Score: "Fine Fishing Song from Haragama" and "Saitara's Song"

Musical Accompaniment 71

music which of these songs was created first and, even in the case of the "en ya do-tio" *kakegoe*, impossible to guess who borrowed what from whom and when. This *kakegoe* is much liked and is used with the "Fine Fishing Song from Haragama" from time to time, as well as with the "Toshima jinku" and the "Kesen-numa jinku" (both from Miyagi).

On the other hand, many songs—such as "the New 'Song of Sōma'"—have very clear musical pedigrees. The "New 'Song of Sōma'" was composed about forty years ago by Suzuki Masao, a native of Sōma and leading folksinger of the day.* Suzuki Masao based the song on older folk songs of Sōma, primarily a version of the "Sōma Barley-hulling Song" for the first half of the melody, and the "Sōma Mowing Song" for the refrain and *kakegoe*. (Ex. 3.)

Ex. 3. Comparative Score: "*Sōma Barley-hulling Song*" and "*New 'Song of Sōma'*"

mugi mo tsuketa shi We've hulled the barley;
negoro mo kita shi bedtime has come;

uchi no oyadachi'a my parents are saying
honto ni nero nero to "Sleep! Sleep!"

"*Sōma Barley-hulling Song*" (*Fukushima*)

*Suzuki Masao is recorded on *NnMY*, Side 6, Item #(61): "Pack-horse man's Song from Sōma." He had a voice of the kind known as "*shibui*"; astringently, quietly beautiful. After his death, his eldest son, who records for Nippon Victor, inherited his name.

| haruka kanata wa | Is that, so far away, |
| Sōma no sora ka yo | the Sōma sky? |

"*New 'Song of Sōma'*" (Fukushima)

According to Matsumoto Keishin, a local Sōma historian, Suzuki Masao also made a minute but significant change in the refrain. He moved the syllable "*to*" from its position before the "*nanda kora yo*" in the "Sōma Mowing Song" and placed it after the "*nanda kora yo*" in the refrain of the "New 'Song of Sōma.'"

"*Nanda kora yo to*" is the proper refrain for the "New 'Song of Sōma,'" and, except in verses where the "*to*" is replaced by another word or syllable, "*to nanda kora yo*" is the proper refrain for the "Sōma Mowing Song." The "*(to)*" in the score below, in the refrain of the "Sōma Mowing Song," is sometimes sung outside of Sōma, but is not sung in Sōma or by singers from Sōma; they treasure the composer's every subtlety. (Ex. 4.)

Ex. 4. *Comparative Score: refrain and* kakegoe *of the "Sōma Mowing Song" and "New 'Song of Sōma'"*

It is possible to see the second half of the melody of the "New 'Song of Sōma'" as a play on the first half, or a development of it. (Ex. 5.)

Ex. 5. From the "New 'Song of Sōma'"

Sōma koishiya How I love Sōma!
natsukashiya   How I miss it!

This is the second half of the verse on the preceding page
"New Song of Sōma" (Fukushima)

While Suzuki Masao did not change the *kakegoe* of the "Sōma Mowing Song," in the "New 'Song of Sōma,'" he made the mood of the *kakegoe* nostalgic rather than whimsical.

Hayashi, or accompaniment by a group of instruments, has two meanings in Japanese folk music. *Hayashi* can be a traditional Japanese festival band, made up of a flute *(fue)*, little gong *(kane)*, and two drums, the *shimedaiko* and the *miya-daiko/o-daiko*. But *hayashi* can also mean the people who perform *hayashi-kotoba*, or the passages in spoken song. *Hayashi-kotoba* (music words or words to accompany by) form longer choruses or responses. Sometimes these are just nonsense words, but, more often than not, they have meaning.

Hayashi-kotoba passages usually have a definite rhythmic pattern, as in the following example from a performance of the "Tanto Song from Tsugaru."* (Ex. 6.)

TMDZS, Side 4, Item #3, second verse. Voice: Ono Ichiko.

Ex. 6. "Tsugaru tanto-bushi" Vocal Score

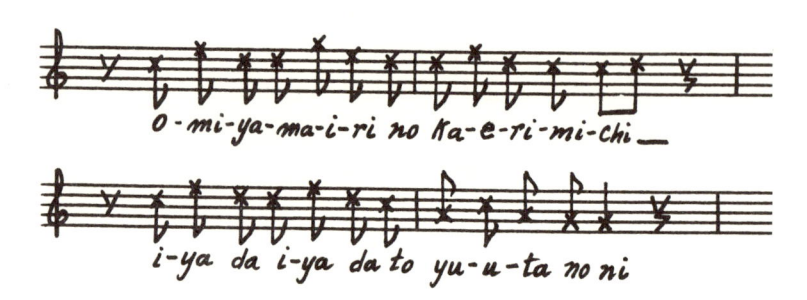

Musical Accompaniment

[musical notation with lyrics:]
O-mi-ya-ma-i-ri no Ka-e-ri-mi-chi
i-ya da i-ya da to yu-u-ta no ni

SONG
so-wa-na-kya shi-nu yo to ta-n-to ta-n-to
nyo-o-bo ni shi-ta to mo
so-no wa- ke da-n yo

ima wa ume-boshi-
babā da keredo
uguisu nakaseta
toki mo aru
toki mo aru
    watashi ga jūku no
    natsu-matsuri
    dondon hanabi no
    ne ni tsurete
    omiya-mairi no
    kaeri-michi
    iya da iya da to
    yūta no ni
sowanak'ya shinu yo to

tanto tanto
nyōbō ni shita to mo
sono wake da n yo

Though now I'm a granny,
a pickled plum,
I've made the nightingale sing
in my time,
in my time!
    At the summer festival
    when I was nineteen,
    taken to the boom-boom
    of the fireworks,
    and, on the way home
    from visiting the shrine,
    even if I did say
    "Don't want to! Don't want to!"
"Marry or die!" was the way it
was, so
tanto tanto
that's the reason they
made me a wife!

"Tanto Song from Tsugaru" (Aomori)

Note that downbeats frequently come on a rest, giving a sense of eight syllables in a seven-syllable line of verse. This strong silent beat is common rhythmical practice in Japanese folk song; it appears in singing and instrumental accompaniments as well as in *hayashi* passages. In traditional Japanese accompaniment, silences and sparseness often have the effect of the drone in East Indian music or harmonization in Western and Black African music. Like *kakegoe*, certain *hayashi-kotoba* may be performed with different voice qualities and rhythms.

There is an entire repertoire of folk songs that is performed half in song and half in *hayashi-kotoba*, including the "*Oiwake* from Shinano" (Nagano) and the "Dance from Awa" (Tokushima). At times, the *hayashi-kotoba* that are sung with the "Oiwake from Shinano," "Toshima *jinku*" (Miyagi), "The Beach Song" (Ibaraki), and others seem to be performed as much for the sake

Ex. 7.   *Examples of* hayashi-kotoba

watashi'a anata ni   I run
tsuite hashiru   after you!

k'ta yo de to ga naru   The door calls, "___ has come!"
dete mirya kaza da yo   When you go and look,
                                              it's the wind!

of sound—the agreeable playing with words—as to convey the meaning of the song. But *hayashi-kotoba* like those for the "Shimoda Song" (Shizuoka), the "Teradomari okesa" (Niigata), or the "Song from Kuma in the *Shamisen's Rokuchōshi* Tuning" (Kumamoto) underline the song's mood, frequently by bringing out a parallel commentary or story.

There are favorite stock lines and verses in *hayashi-kotoba*, such as (Ex. 7.)

On the other hand, many *hayashi-kotoba* are improvised on the spur of the moment, for a particular occasion. Sometimes, too, singers stretch a stanza, putting an additional phrase of poetry to the melody.

A number of "talking songs" are completely in *hayashi-kotoba;* perhaps "Akita ondo" is the most famous. Talking songs are fast songs and, like the idiot's band music, are perfect for drinking, dancing, and coquetting. So in the sixties and seventies, talking songs were as popular in Japanese bars as they were at old-fashioned Japanese banquets. Bar hostesses, generally known as "the poor man's geisha," seemed to enjoy a well-turned compliment in *hayashi-kotoba* as much as one from the latest hit song.

From the earliest written examples of Japanese song lyrics, in the *Kojiki* and other works, we can see that both *hayashi-kotoba* and *kakegoe* have been rooted in Japanese folk song since ancient times. In the twentieth century, they continue to appeal as musical and poetic techniques and as manifestations, however casually expressed, of a traditional view of the arts—a divine creation, generously extended to mankind for our use, a bridge on which the divine and the human can meet in safety, with affection.

The instrumental accompaniment of Japanese folk song is as varied as its vocal accompaniment, and as flexible. One dramatic example of a single musical instrument's capacity to develop and expand continuously is the shamisen. Within less than a century after its introduction in Japan, the shamisen had become essential to Japanese folk song, as well as central in Kabuki and Bunraku theater music and more than a dozen different old and new popular song styles. Among Japanese instruments, only the *shakuhachi*, in its lively and aggressive adaptations of other instruments' repertoires, comes near the shamisen.

By the 1980s, thanks to Japanese movies, some of the many styles of folk shamisen had become internationally famous. The composer Satō Masaru used Tsugaru shamisen music in the score for the desperado-movie "The Wolves"* and reached a wide audience in American and Europe, in love with the martial arts. Other Japanese sword-fighting movies shown abroad have also featured folk shamisen played geisha style as part of their background music. Among examples of these movies are several of the film versions of "The Loyal Forty-Seven Rōnin" ("Chūshingura") and the epic series about the samurai artist, strategist, and Buddhist monk, Miyamoto Musashi. So when local artists from Aomori Prefecture, the home of Tsugaru folk music, toured America in 1975 and 1976, they were met with a warm reception and an audience that had already been exposed to the pyrotechnics of the Tsugaru shamisen.

The Tsugaru shamisen is larger than the shamisen normally used to accompany Japanese folk songs. The player follows the singer's flamboyant, highly-decorated melody run for run and ornament for ornament, but periodically takes off on his own fireworks display also. Tsugaru shamisen pieces may be compared to Bach's chorale preludes for the organ; they are related to specific songs but can also be solo works. The Tsugaru shamisen style and many of the songs associated with it eventually spread to Hokkaidō, but there, although the playing is as fast, the sound and feeling are lighter.

Throughout Japan, many folk songs provide opportunities for virtuoso passages on the shamisen. Usually these come in the introduction to the song, as in the "Song from Yasugi" (Shimane), the "Ondo from Takayama" (Gifu), or the "Song from Kuma in the Shamisen's Rokuchōshi Tuning" (Kumamoto). But occasionally the shamisen's solo occurs partway through a song, as in "Esashi oiwake" (Hokkaidō).

For Ryūkyūan dances and songs, people still play the *sanshin*, the Chinese-Ryūkyūan ancestor of the Japanese shamisen.

*Original title: "Shussho no o-iwai" ("Celebration on Release from Prison"). The movie starred the famous actor Tatsuya Nakadai; one of the costars was renowned as an exdesperado of the kind portrayed in the film.

Although it influenced Japanese folk shamisen music, most directly in Kagoshima, Nagasaki, and other southern prefectures, the Ryukyuan/Okinawan folk *sanshin* repertoire is distinct from the folk shamisen repertoire of the four main islands of Japan.

In Japanese folk song, there are three basic ways to tune the strings of a shamisen (Ex. 8.):

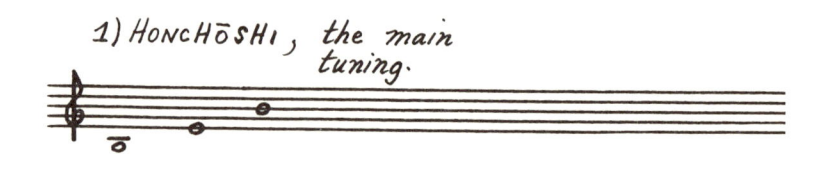

1) HONCHŌSHI, the main tuning.

2) NI-AGARI, tuning with the second string raised a step

3) SAN-SAGURI, tuning with the third string lowered a step

Ex. 8.   Basic Shamisen Tunings

Some folk songs have versions distinguished by the particular way in which the strings of the accompanying shamisen are tuned. Thus, the "Song from Shinjo" (Yamagata) is distinguished from the " 'Song from Shinjo' in Ni-agari Tuning" (Yamagata). In addition, there are individual folk songs all over Japan known by the shamisen tunings *san-sagari* and *ni-agari*. *San-sagari* and *ni-agari* are performed at parties by geisha and other professional entertainers. Usually each *san-sagari* and *ni-agari* is named after its place of origin, as "The *San-sagari* from Kagoshima" (Kagoshima) or the "Song in *Ni-agari* Tuning from Mito" (Ibaraki). Perhaps the title indicated the presence of skilled shamisen players in the area.

The character of the shamisen accompaniment is influenced by a song's origins. A folk song from an old entertainment quarter, popular among geisha for a hundred years, may have a very sparse, apparently casual shamisen behind it, the accompaniment consisting of isolated notes or phrases taken from the singer's melody with the rhythm unemphasized. The party-style folk song "Pickled Plum" (Saga) is an example of this approach. Minimal accompaniment is also found in old popular-song genres such as the *ko-uta* and the *dodoitsu* (city ditty).

On the other hand, the shamisen can go to the opposite extreme. In the songs from Tsugaru, it sticks to the singer's melody as closely as a flute or another voice. Or the shamisen's melody may weave in and out of the singer's melody, as in the "Ondo from Takayama" (Gifu).

In a large number of pieces—party songs such as "A Song on Three Levels" (Niigata) and the "Shimoda Song" (Shizuoka), for example—the singer performs in one key, the shamisen in another (using Western-influence terminology; the Japanese originals were composed according to a different system).

In songs such as "The Dance from Awa" (Tokushima), the shamisen acts as part of the percussion, repeating the same rhythmic pattern under the singer's melody. And in other songs such as the "Ballad from Aikawa" (Niigata: Sado Island), the shamisen plays a long recurring melodic pattern under the singer's melody and independent of it.

Since it is capable of such enormous range, it is no wonder the shamisen is as important to Japanese folk song as the violin is to Middle Eastern popular music.

Two more stringed instruments—the *koto* and the *kokyu*—are also used to accompany folk songs, although they have much larger repertoires in other types of music.

The *koto*, a zither that usually has thirteen strings, is not really a folk instrument, either in Japan proper or in the Ryūkyū Islands. However, there are arrangements with *koto* for several southern Japanese folk songs, including the "Oiwake from Bungo," also known as "The Kujū Plateau" (Ōita), and

"Tabaruzaka" (Kumamoto). In such arrangements, the *koto* serves to establish a nostalgic mood of ancient courtly life.

The *kokyū*, a four-stringed member of the viol family, in appearance is similar to the Indonesian *rebab* and the Chinese *erh-hu*. Like the shamisen, the *kokyū*'s history is rooted in the entertainment district, but nowadays, in folk music, the *kokyū* is associated primarily with specific dances and their accompanying songs, such as the "owara-song from Etchū" (Toyama) and the "Dance from Tsurusaki" (Oita). The *kokyū* also accompanies songs from the islands south of Kagoshima and in the Ryūkyūs, along with the *koto* and the *sanshin* or *shamisen*.

Woodwinds—specifically flutes—play an even greater part in Japanese folk song than do stringed instruments. The most typical woodwinds that are used in folk music are the *shakuhachi* and the *fue*.

The *shakuhachi* is used with other instruments to accompany many folk songs. But *shakuhachi* players have developed their own folk specialty also, which is a solo instrumental accompaniment to slow, ornamented songs, including "Esashi oiwake," many boatmen's songs, most of the packhorsemen's songs, and the slow congratulation songs. Musicians or aficionados call this music *take-mono*, meaning songs accompanied only by the bamboo *(take) shakuhachi*. Such accompaniment is a variation on the singer's melody that reinforces and comments on it.

The Japanese bamboo flute, the *fue* (specifically, *take-bue* or *shino-bue*), accompanies both Buddhist and Shintō festival songs and dances. It is probably one of the oldest folk instruments in Japan.

Percussion, too, holds a fundamental place in Japanese folk music.

Members of the rattle and scraper group of percussion instruments, the *sasara* group which includes such instruments as the *bin-zasara*, are connected with religious festival music and dances such as the Akita "Dance of Daikoku the God of Wealth." The *suri-zasara*, a scratcher instrument much like the Latin American guiro, is very common in the Kantō region.

There are also at least three sizes of gongs *(kane)*, but the smallest (hand-size) and the middle-sized ones are used most often to accompany folk songs and dances. These instruments are often called *chanchiki* or *changiri* after their mnemonics.

The four drums that are typically played in folk-song and folk-dance music are the *taiko*, the *shime-daiko*, the *miya-daiko/ō-daiko* and the *okedō*. The *taiko* is the smallest of the four and, like the *shime-daiko*, which is also small, its heads and body are held together by ropes. The *miya-daiko* is a larger drum and is shaped like a beer keg. When used as a shrine or festival drum, the *miya-daiko* can take a terrific beating and can be heard well over a mile in the open air. The *okedō* is also large but is tubular-shaped and is played with thin drumsticks. Drums other than these four are also used at times, especially the large or small hour-glass-shaped drums, the *tsuzumi*.

In record notes, *kane* and percussion other than drums are often referred to simply as *narimono* or, literally, things that sound.

Almost all of these Japanese folk-musical instruments also have or have had repertoires in art music, theater and popular music, and religious music. Many shamisen players who perform folk music, for instance, also play *ha-uta* or *ji-uta*, Kabuki or doll-puppet theater music, and other traditional genres. Many players of folk *shakuhachi* also play "classical" *shakuhachi; fue* players may be jazz musicians as well. Japanese folk music has always been intertwined with the many other varieties of traditional and modern music in that country.

Chapter Six
The Present-Day Musical Mixture

ALTHOUGH OLD OR OLD-STYLE Japanese folk songs can be written down, divided into measures, and given a key signature, it is more common for these songs to be organized by melodic or rhythmic pattern, phrase, a structure or structures in the poetry, or by cycles of beats, rather than by a given meter, in a key or mode.

On the other hand, the melodies of many modern Japanese folk songs show a heavy Western musical influence. Unlike older songs, they are frequently in major or minor keys, and, consequently, are comparatively easy to arrange for orchestra or band. The rhythms are usually much simpler when compared to the complex, subtle rhythmic patterns of many of the older Japanese folk songs. The meter is a regular 2/4, 4/4 or 3/4, and the form and phrasing of pieces such as "The Factory-girls' Song" (Ex. 9.) show the influence of Western musical theory. These qualities have made it possible for the "Flowered Hat Dance" (Yamagata) and the "Northern Kyūshū Coal-miner's Song" (an old song from Fukuoka that has been considerably simplified in this century)* to be adopted without reservation by American children in summer camps and Americans living in Japan.

---

*See Migita, 51; Machida-Asano, 326; NnMY, Side 17, Items #(149) and #(150). Voices: Hoshino Tamiko; Akasaka Ko-ume.

The Present-Day Musical Mixture 85

jokō jokō to "Women workers! Factory wenches!"
misageru na Don't look down on us!
joko-san no tsumetaru The canned goods
kanzume wa made by factory women
Yokohama tensa de pass the inspection
gōkaku shi at Yokohama
joko-san no homare de and are sent to foreign lands
gaikoku e with praise for the women workers.

Ex. 9. *The Factory Girls' Song" (Hokkaidō)*

But it isn't just the melodies that have been influenced by Western music. While traditional instruments are still popular, Japanese folk songs are also accompanied by Western military bands, Western orchestras, jazz combos, and Western instruments such as pianos and guitars. Mixtures of Japanese and Western musical styles and instruments have been part of the Japanese musical scene since the 1880s.

Orchestral accompaniment greatly affects the nature of a folk song. The delicately sensual Kyōto folk song, "Melody from Miyazu," if accompanied by *taiko*, shamisen and *fue*, sounds like a typical, sophisticated, Japanese party-style folk song. When the same song is accompanied by shamisen and Western orchestra or band, a feeling of nostalgia overwhelms any sophistication, and a raffish quality becomes more apparent—although the words remain unchanged.*

A guitar, strummed with a flat pick or the fingers, is sometimes substituted for a lighter shamisen sound or for *koto*. For example, the top three guitar strings can be tuned in *honchōshi*, *ni-agari* or *san-sagari*, the three basic shamisen tunings, and the fourth string can be tuned an octave below the second string. (The bottom two strings are damped to prevent jarring overtones.) But it is more common to play the old melodies on a guitar Western-style, over Western harmonies. The banjo, too, is fairly common in Japan, due to the enormous popularity of bluegrass and country and western music. A shamisen player thoroughly enjoys picking "The Wabash Cannonball" on the shamisen and then switching to a Tsugaru breakdown on the banjo.

In addition, there is a constant give and take among the *shakuhachi*, the *kokyū* (Japanese viol), and the Western violin; and the trumpet and saxophone share the role of backbone in the *enka* band with the *shakuhachi*. Western-style flutists always have their ears open for Japanese *shakuhachi* techniques; in turn, many *shakuhachi* and *fue* players are tremendously excited by jazz. Recorders in all sizes can play *fue* and *shakuhachi* music, and the soprano recorder has become a standard instrument in Japanese primary schools.

*For example, compare the shamisen, *fue*, *taiko*-accompanied performance of Tachibana Tamae (King LP LKF 1042, Side 1, Item #4) with the orchestra and shamisen-accompanied performance of Mihashi Michiya (King LP KR 15, Side 1, Item #3).

Jazz and Latin bands play Bon-Festival music, though not usually at the Bon Festival. But, at times, the traditional Bon-Dance band now includes an accordion or some other Western instrument. When singing in bars or at parties, people use anything handy for percussion: silverware, chopsticks on a glass or ricebowl, the lid of a pot. Anything that makes a good noise is fine. Of course, jazz and Latin drums can play Japanese drum music, with maracas and guiros echoing the Japanese rattles and scrapers, and a triangle or claves can follow the Japanese hand gongs *(kane)*.

This lively trade between Eastern and Western musical techniques is continuing to grow, with the probability of more exchanges and the development of even newer techniques ever on the horizon. As just one example, the whole area of exchange between Japanese and Middle Eastern music is wide open and full of possibilities.

Since about 1890, a major addition to the Japanese folk-song repertoire has been the *shin min'yō* (the new-style folk song), an increasingly sophisticated blend of Japanese and Western music. Among its functions, the *shin min'yō* provides local places with the souvenir songs that have been a staple of Japanese folk song since ancient times.

When Japan reopened contact with the Western world in the 1860s, Western culture was welcomed wholeheartedly, apparently with a total lack of reserve. Some people regard the Meiji Era (1868–1912) as another renaissance in Japanese culture, while others see it as a time when Japan was almost overcome by insidious occidentals and their works. The folk songs of the Meiji (1868–1912), Taishō (1912–1926), and early Shōwa (1926–) Eras reflect the stresses and vitality of those changing times. They are songs with lyrics of newly revived classical Chinese and Japanese poems that have been set to hymnlike tunes. These are the songs of people who grew up with missionary, military, and jazz band music, or orchestral and choral music, as much a part of their musical world as the shamisen, if not more so. This is the music of a people whose world was suddenly changed in thousands of small and large ways and who needed to find an acceptable balance.

During the four hundred years after its introduction from China via the Ryūkyū Islands, the shamisen became part of the Japanese folk-instrument tradition. Then in the nineteenth century, *shakuhachi* players developed a repertoire of folk song—the *take-mono*, integrating traditional Japanese folk songs into the repertoires of Japanese popular and jazz singers. In another century, or perhaps even in this century, the clarinet or the accordion may become a permanent fixture in Japanese folk-song accompaniment. The clarinet already has a place in folk music in the *chindonya*, the one- or two-man band that advertises the opening of a store, coffee-house, pinball parlor, etc.

Since a tendency to borrow, assimilate, and change is so characteristic of the world of folk music, it is not suprising that Japanese folksingers and musicians have drawn new instruments into their body of sound. At the same time, older songs and ways of composing them continue to flourish side by side with the new style songs (some of which are at least fifty years old), but, as in the past, with perhaps new verses and different arrangements. In Japanese folk song, things have a tendency to change, but nothing ever really dies out.

Discography

Although the following list is confined to the songs cited in the text, there are over a thousand well-known Japanese folk songs available on commercial recordings.

Recordings of Japanese folk songs, including both scholarly recordings and popular versions and arrangements, can be found in department stores like Takashimaya and Mitsukoshi, as well as in most record shops and instrument stores in any large city in Japan.

Major producers of folk-song records, tapes, and cassettes are Nippon Columbia, Nippon Victor, the Japan Broadcasting Corporation (NHK), Toshiba, and King. Among other Japanese record companies that issue important folk-song recordings are Teichiku, Crown, Polydor, and Minoruphon.

Most recordings contain song texts and large albums usually include substantial booklets. In addition to song texts, many records contain movement-by-movement sketches or photographs of the dances.

Although most Japanese recordings list all performers' names, only the names of the principal singers are given here, as in Japanese record catalogues.

Abbreviations

Columbia   Nippon Columbia Records
King   King Records

MGRK	Min'yō gen'ryū-kō—Esashi oiwake to Sado okesa A detailed study primarily of "Esashi oiwake" and "Sado okesa" but with notes on the "Aiya!/Haiya! Song," the *ni-agari* and *sansagari*, and many other types of Japanese folk song. Columbia LP AL-5047 to AL-5050 (four records)
NHK	The tape cassette series issued by NHK, the Japan Broadcasting Corporation—"Furusato no uta" (Songs From Back Home). Nine tape cassettes, with booklets including song texts enclosed.
NHK-R	A series of books, with compact LPs inserted in them. Issued by NHK in 1968–69. Nine volumes. (Also entitled "Furusato no uta.")
NnMY	Nihon no min'yō (Folk Songs of Japan) A general survey of Japanese folk song, including that of the Ryukyus. Edited by Machido Kashō, the album includes a booklet (in Japanese) that contains the song texts, singers' and musicians' names, background notes, maps, and illustrations. Columbia LP AL-4118 to AL-4127 (ten records)
Rōsaku	Nihon rōsaku min'yō shūsei—ikite ita hataraku hito-tachi no utagoe (A Collection of Folk Songs of Japanese Workers—the Living Voices of Laboring People) An in-depth study of Japanese work songs of many kinds, including farming, factory, mining, and lumbering songs. The album was produced for the Nineteenth Festival of the Arts held in 1964 and was edited by Machida Kashō. A booklet containing song texts, singers' names, and photographs is enclosed. Victor LP JV-158 to JV-163 (six records)

Discography

Shimokita	*Nihon no kyōdo geino*—*Shimokita hantō o tazunete* (Rural Performing Arts of Japan—an Inquiry on the Shimokita Peninsula) An excellent record of folk songs, religious ritual songs, and music from a local folk Nō theater from the Nambu Region in Aomori. The modern, on-the-spot recordings have commentary by Tōyō Ongaku Gakkai. Columbia LP AL–5044
Teichiku	Teichiku Records
TF	A Toshiba Records series of six single-record LP albums (TR–6010 to TR–6015)—"Furusato no uta—Nihon min'yō-shū" (Songs from Back Home—An Anthology of Japanese Folk Songs). Title in English: "Folk Songs of Japan."
TMDZS	*Tōhoku min'yō daizenshū* (Complete Collection of Folk Songs of the Northeast) A collection of many of the best-known songs from northeast Japan, featuring many local professional and semiprofessional folksingers. In addition to song texts, background notes, and names of singers and instrumentalists, the booklet contains a large photographic section showing the movements to the dance songs included in the album, as performed by various well-known dancers such as Hanayanagi Shū, Nishizaki Midori II, and Wakayanagi Takami. Columbia LP–DLS–4201 to DLS–4210; TD–3005 (eleven records)
Toshiba	Toshiba Records other than the above series.
Victor	Nippon Victor Records

"Agarashare" ("Come Right In"), Yamagata
   NnMY Side 6, Item #52
       Voice: Itō Kazuko

"Aikawa ondo" ("Ballad from Aikawa"), Niigata: Sado Island
    Toshiba 45 rpm TP–1670
        Voice: Hamada Kiichi (II)
    Victor 45 rpm MV–56
        Voice (alternating):
            Sugiyama Mozaemon
            Okako Jūtarō
            Ikeda Shigeo
    NnMY Side 10, Item #90
        Voice: Murata Bunzō
    NHK No. 6, Item #2
        Voices (alternating):
            Tatsunami-kai (The Rising Waves Society)

"Ajigasa jinku," Aomori
    Victor 45 rpm MV–551–S
        Voice: Asari Miki

"Aki no yama-uta" ("Autumn Song for Work in the Mountains"), Miyagi
    NnMY Side 3, Item #29
        Voice: Kumagaya Kazuo

"Akita Daikoku-Mai" ("Dance of Daikoku, the God of Wealth"), Akita
    TMDZS Side 5, Item #5
        Voice: Sasaki Tsuneo

"Akita jinku," Akita
    Toshiba 45 rpm TP–1759
        Voice: Asano Chizuko

"Akita ondo," Akita
    Columbia 45 rpm SAS–6083
        Voice: Sasaki Haruko
    TMDZS Side 5, Item #1
        Voice: Ono Hanako

"Akita usu-hiki-uta" ("An Akita Miller's Song"), Akita
    Toshiba 45 rpm TP–1598
        Voice: Sumida Masataka

  TMDZS Side 7, Item #7
   Voice: Satō Sawae

"Anko-bushi" ("Song of the Pretty Girls"), Tōkyō: Oshima
 NHK No. 5. Item #11
  Voice: Oshima (O-)Riki

"Awa no mugi-uchi-uta" ("Grain-pounding Song
 from Awa"), Tokushima
  Toshiba 45 rpm TP-1376
   Voice: Hamada Kiichi (II)
  Columbia 45 rpm SAS-6294
   Voice: Harumi Yōko

"Awa odori" ("The Dance from Awa"), Tokushima
 MGRK Side 3-A, Item #(b)4
  Voice (alternating):
   Wakita Tamano
   Izumiya Toshiko
   Nii Misa
 Victor 45 rpm MV-565-S
  Voice: Mineno Toshiko

"[Bitchū] Matsuyama odori" ("The Matsuyama Dance"
 in Bitchū Province), Okayama
  Columbia 45 rpm SA-1179
   Voice: Murata Hideo

"Chakkiri-bushi" ("Tea-Cutters' Song"), Shizuoka
 Words: Kitahara Hakushū
 Music: Machida Kashō
  Toshiba 45 rpm TP-1732
   Voice: Minemura Toshimisa

"Esashi oiwake" ("Packhorseman's Art Song
 from Esashi"), Hokkaidō
  Columbia LP DLS-4122:
   "Esashi oiwake taikai" ("Esashi oiwake tournament")
  King LP KR95:
   "Esashi oiwake kyōen-shu" ("Collection of Esashi
   oiwake recital competitions")

Teichiku LP NL–2532:
"Esashi oiwake meijin taikai" ("Tournament by famous performers of Esashi oiwake")

MGRK (A study of the origins and development of "Esashi oiwake")

"Etchū owara-bushi" ("The Owara Song from Etchū"), Toyama

Columbia 45 rpm SA–250
Voices: Members of the Toyama Prefecture Folk-Song Owara Conservation Society
Solo Voice: (Side 1) Eki Yukuo
(Side 2) Fukushima Sakuichi

"Gōshū ondo" ("Ballad from Ōmi"), Shiga

NnMY Side 13, Item #118
Voice: Sakuragawa Umeo

Teichiku LP NL–2106
Voice: Sakuragawa Umeo

"Hakata-bushi" ("Song from Hakata"), Fukuoka

NnMY Side 17, Item #145
Voice: Akasaka Ko-ume

King 45 rpm BS–5013
Voice: Kikutarō

"Hanagasa odori"/"Hanagasa ondo" ("The Flowered Hat Dance"), Yamagata

King LP KR 13 Side 2, Item #5
Voice: Mihashi Michiya

NHK No. 3, Item #19
Voice: Satō Katsue

"Haragama tairyō-bushi" ("Fine Fishing Song from Haragama"), Fukushima: Sōma

TMDZS Side 19, Item #6
Voice: Kibata Kunio

"Hitachi dodoitsu" ("City Ditty from Hitachi"), Ibaraki

TF TR–6014 Side 1, Item #9
Voice: Fukuda Yūko

Discography

"Hokkai san-sagari," Hokkaidō
> *King* 45 rpm BS-5257
> Voice: Sasaki Motoharu

"Iso-bushi" ("The Beach Song"), Ibaraki
> *NnMY* Side 7, Item #67
> Voice: Miyoju/Miyosu
>
> *Victor* 45 rpm MV-82
> Voice: Mito Kikue
>
> *NHK* No. 5, Item #2
> Voice: Sekine Yoshi

"Isohara-bushi" ("Song from Isohara"), Ibaraki
> *Columbia* 45 rpm SAS-6266
> Voice: Harumi Yōko

"It-cha-it-cha-bushi" ("*It-cha-It-cha* Song"), Chiba
> *Victor* 45 rpm MV-524-S
> Voice: Hamada Kiichi (I)

"Itsuki no komori-uta" ("Nursemaid's Song from Itsuki Village"/"Lullaby from Itsuki Village"), Kumamoto
> party-song version, known nationwide:
> *NnMY* Side 18, Item #160
> Voice: Kikutarō
>
> local version:
> *NHK* No. 9, Item #8
> Voice: Dōzaka Yoshiko

"Jokō-bushi" ("The Factory-Girls' Song"), Hokkaidō
> *King* LP KR 52 Side 2, Item #8
> Voice: Hanamura Junko/Sachiko

"Kagoshima ohara-bushi" ("The Ohara Song from Kagoshima"), Kagoshima
> *King* LP KR 15 Side 2, Item #8
> Voice: Hiyama Sakura
>
> *NnMY* Side 20, Item #168
> Voice: Komaki Kikue

NHK No. 9, Item #15
Voices: members of the Kagoshima Folk Arts Company

"Kagoshima san-sagari" ("*San-sagari* from Kagoshima"), Kagoshima

NHK No. 9, Item #16
Voices: jimoto yūji (local volunteers)

"Kakuma-kari-uta" ("Tree-pruning Song"), Yamagata

TMDZS Side 14, Item #7
Voice: Akagi Saburō

"Kanchororin-bushi" ("The *Kanchororin* Song"), Fukushima: Sōma

Sōma style:
TMDZS Side 22, Item #4
Voice: Momonoi Kasei

Tōkyō style:
King LP KR–36 Side 1, Item #2
Voice: Kaga Tokuko

"Kari-boshi-kiri-uta" ("Reed-Cutters' Song"), Miyazaki

Columbia LP DLS–4116 Side 2, Item #1

Voice: Harumi Yōko

TF TR–6014 Side 2, Item #9
Voice: Satō Akira

"Kawachi ondo" ("Ballad from Kawachi"), Ōsaka

Victor LP MC–85–S
Voice: (Side 1) Hatsuin'ya Kenji
(Side 2) Hatsuin'ya Tasaburō

Columbia LP DLS–4157
Voice: Hatsuin'ya Kenji

Columbia 45 rpm SAS–6038
Voice: Miyoshiya Hajime

Columbia LP DLS–4244
Voice: (Side 1) Ikoma Hajime
(Side 2) Ikoma Manabu

"Kenryō-bushi" ("Kenryō's Song"), Aomori
   Columbia 45 rpm SAS–6030
      Voice: Asari Miki
   Toshiba 45 rpm TP-1720
      Voice: Yamamoto Kenji

"Kesen-numa jinku," Miyagi
   TMDZS Side 18, Item #1
      Voice: Kibata Kunio

"Kita Kyūshū tanko-bushi" ("Northern Kyushu Coal-Miners' Song"), Fukuoka
   local version:
   NnMY Side 17, Item #149
      Voice: Hoshine Tamiko
   party-song version, known nationwide
   NnMY Side 17, Item #150
      Voice: Akasaka Ko-ume

"Komoro mago-uta" ("Packhorse-Man's Song from Komoro"), Nagano
   Columbia 45 rpm SAS–6274
      Voice: Akasaka Ko-ume
   Toshiba 45 rpm TP–1680
      Voice: Hamada Kiichi (II)

"Kotsu-kotsu-bushi" ("The 'Knock-Knock!' Song"), Ōita
   King LP SS–5045
      Voice: Kikutarō

"Dōnan kudoki-bushi" (a wooing song), Hokkaidō
   NHK No. 1, Item #11
      Voice: Sasaki Motoharu

"Kujū kogen" ("The Kujū Plateau"), Ōita
   King LP SS–5045
      Voice: Satō Matsuko
   Toshiba LP TR–6075 Side 1, Item #5
      Voice: Hamada Kiichi (II)

98   Discography

"Kuma (no) rokuchōshi" ("The Song from Kuma in the Shamisen's *Rokuchoshi* Tuning"), Kumamoto

   King LP SEM 37 Side 2, Item #4
      Voice: Nishi Hiroyuki

   TF TR–6015 Side 2, Item #8
      Voice: Hamada Kiichi (II)

   NnMY Side 18, Item #161
      Voice: Fujimoto Isuzu

   NHK No. 9, Item #9
      Voice (and *kakegoe* and *hayashi*):
      Members of the Kuma Folk-Song
      Conservation Society

   MGRK Side 3–A, Item #(a)3
      Voice: Koyama Shōsei

"Kuroda-bushi" ("Song of the Kuroda Warriors"), Fukuoka

   Columbia 45 rpm SA–592
      Voice: Akasaka Ko-ume

"Matsumae san-sagari" ("*San-sagari* from Matsumae"), Hokkaidō

   Toshiba 45 rpm TP–1565
      Voice: Hamada Kiichi (II)

"Mito no ni-agari" ("Song in the *Ni-agari* Tuning from Mito"), Ibaraki

   Toshiba 45 rpm TP–1475
      Voice: Fukuda Yūko

"Miyazu-bushi"/"Tango no Miyazu-bushi" ("Melody from Miyazu"), Kyōto

   King LP LKF 1042 Side 1, Item #4
      Voice: Tachibana Tamae

   King LP KR 15 Side 1, Item #3
      Voice: Mihashi Michiya

"Mugi ya-bushi" ("The Barley-and-Such Song"), Toyama

   NnMY Side 11, Item #97
      Voices (alternating):
         Kuri Kikuji/Kikuharu
         Nakamura Matsuemon

Nagamochi-uta (trousseau-carrying songs) Miyagi

NHK No. 4, Item #5
Voice: Akama Masao (Rinsui)

King 45 rpm BS-5105
Voice: Mihashi Michiya

Toshiba 45 rpm TP-1758
Voice: Asano Chizuko

Victor 45 rpm MV-259
Voice: Miura Kimiko

"Naga mugi-ya" ("Long Version of 'The Barley-and-Such Song'"), Toyama

NnMY Side 12, Item #98
Voices: members of the Etchū Province Gokayama Village "Barley-and-Such Song" Conservation Society

"Nambu dodoitsu" ("The City Ditty from Nambu"), Aomori

Toshiba 45 rpm TP-1235
Voice: Natsuzaka Kikuo

NKG-S Side 2, Item #2
Voices (alternating):
Kawakami Shige
Miyamoto Shiwa

"Nambu ushikata-bushi" ("Cowherd's Song from Nambu"), Aomori

TMDZS Side 4, Item #2
Voice: Tatematsu Eiki

"Nanao Madara" ("The Madara Island Song from Nanao"). Ishikawa

NnMY Side 11, Item #101
Voices: Maehama Shintarō
Nanao City Yada District Young Men's Association

"Ni-agari Shinjo-bushi" ("'Song from Shinjo' in *Ni-agari* Tuning"), Yamagata

Toshiba 45 rpm TP-1672
Voice: Minemura Toshimisa

"Niishima it-cha-bushi" ("Niishima *It-cha* Song"), Tōkyō: Oshima

   King LP SKM 17 Side 2, Item #6
   Voice: Aonuma

"Niitsu jinku," Niigata

   TF TR–6015 Side 2, Item #2
   Voice: Ko-uta Katsutarō

"Nora sangai-bushi" ("Rural 'Song on Three Levels'"), Niigata

   NHK No. 6, Item #6
   Voice: Izumi Maki

"Oiwake kuzushi," Hokkaidō

   MGRK Side 1–B, Items #4, 5
   Voice: Abe Shōzan

"Oiwake mago-uta" ("Packhorseman's Song from Oiwake"), Nagano

   MGRK Side 1–A, Item #1
   or
   NHK No. 7, Item #4
   Voice: Ogawa Sei'ichirō

"Ōtsu-e-bushi" ("Ōtsu-Picture Song"), Shiga

   Victor LP MC–44
   Voice: Kimie (probably a geisha)
   NnMY Side 7, Item #65
   Voice: Yamanouchi Bansui*

"Ringo-bushi" ("Apple Song"), Aomori
Composed by Narita Un'chiku.

   Victor 45 rpm MV–560–S
   Voice: Asari Miki

---

   *Here recorded as "Aizu Ōtsu-e," which is a congratulation song from Aizu in Fukushima. However, this is a performance of the Shiga Ōtsu-e music, with a narrative text, as is usual in Shiga.
   An example of "Aizu Ōtsu-e" as a congratulation song with a local melody is: King LP KR 35, Side 1, Item #3; Voice: Utagawa Shigeo.

"Sado okesa," Niigata: Sado Island
   MGRK Side 4-B, Item #10
      Voice: Murata Bunzō

"Sangai-bushi" ("A Song on Three Levels")
   Niigata: Kashiwazaki
   King LP LKF 1041 Side 2, Item #3
      Voice: Yanagiya Yume

"Sanjukkokubune funa-uta" ("Thirty-Bushel Cargo Boat Song"), Osaka
   NnMY Side 14, Item #121
      Voices: Kondō Tanzan
              Kondō Masahiro
   King 45 rpm BS-5209
      Voice: Yoshizara Hiroshi
   NHK No. 8, Item #4
      Voice: Ikeda Senjirō

"Sansa shigure" ("Late Autumn Rain"), Miyagi, Fukushima, Iwate
   King LP KR 13, Side 2, Item#1
      Voice: Watanabe Ayako

"Seichō Hakata-bushi" ("Traditional 'Song from Hakata'"), Fukuoka
   NnMY Side 17, Item #146
      Voice: Hakata Rōshō/Oimatsu/Oyumatsu
   King LP LKF-1043 Side 1, Item # 1
      Voice: Hakata Fujie

"Shimoda-bushi" ("The Shimoda Song"), Shizuoka
   MGRK Side 3-b, Item #20
      Voice. Ogawa Tan'ryū
   NHK No. 7, Item #11
      Voices (two, alternating
         from a group of Shimoda *geigi*)
   Toshiba 45 rpm TP-1159
      Voice: Hamada Kiichi (II)

Discography

"Shinano oiwake," Nagano
> *Victor* 45 rpm MV–545–S
> Voice: Hamada Kiichi (I)
>
> *Toshiba* LP TR–6075 Side 2, Item #2
> Voice: Hamada Kiichi (II)

"Shin Hokkai bon-uta" ("New 'Bon-Festival Song from Hokkaido'"), Hokkaidō
> *King* 45 rpm BS–5307
> Voice: Fujita Shūjirō

"Shinjo-bushi" ("Song from Shinjo"), Yamagata
> *Toshiba* 45 rpm TP–1219
> Voice: Tsuji Masami

"Shin sansa shigure" ("New 'Late Autumn Rain'"), Miyagi
Words and Music: Takeda Chūichirō
> *TMDZS* Side 17, Item #2
> Voice: Saeki Chieko

"Shin Sōma-bushi" ("New 'Song of Sōma'"), Fukushima
Suzuki Masao (the Elder)
> *TMDZS* Side 20, Item #4
> Voice: Endō Yukimori
>
> *NHK* No. 4, Item #13
> Voice: Hangae Jōsei

"Shin *tanto*-bushi" ("New '*Tanto* Song'"), Akita
> *King* 45 rpm BS–5033
> Voice: Harada Naoyuki
>
> *King* 45 rpm BS–5051
> Voice: Saitō Keiko

"Shōnai obako" ("Shōnai Belle"), Yamagata
> *Columbia* 45 rpm SAS–6241
> Voice: Sekimoto Tomiko

"Sōma bon-uta" ("Bon Song from Sōma"), Fukushima
> *TMDZS* Side 20, Item #3
> Voice: Hangae Jōsei

"Sōma-bushi" ("Song of Sōma"), Fukushima
TMDZS Side 19, Item #3
Voice: Momonoi Kasei

"Sōma kusa-kari-uta" ("Sōma Mowing Song")
TMDZS Side 22, Item #2
Voice: Kibata Kunio

"Sōma mago-uta" ("Packhorseman's Song from Sōma"), Fukushima
NnMY Side 6, Item #61
Voice: Suzuki Masao (the Elder)

"Sōma mugi-tsuki-uta" ("Sōma Barley-hulling Song"), Fukushima
TMDZS Side 21, Item #1
Voice: Hangae Jōsei

Rōsaku, record no. JV-159(B), Item #84
Voice: Ogoshi Toraaki

___ Item #85 (Northern Sōma style)
Voice: Sugimoto Sakao

"Sōma Nagareyama" ("The Nagareyama Song"), Fukushima
TMDZS Side 20, Item #2
Voice: Ogoshi Nobuyuki

NnMY Side 6, Item #56
Voice: Ara Fuyo

King LP KR 36 Side 2, Item #1
Voice: Yoshizawa Hiroshi

"Sōma nihengaeshi" ("The Refrain from Sōma"), Fukushima

Northern Sōma style *(kita-kata)*:
TMDZS Side 21, Item #2
Voice: Abe Ichirō

Southern Sōma style *(minami-kata)*:
TMDZS Side 19, Item #1
Voice: Endō Yukimori

"*Sōran*-bushi" ("The *Sōran* Song"), Hokkaidō

> *King* LP KR 52 Side *1, Item* #1 (under the title "Oki-age *soran*-bushi")
> Voice: Kamata Eiichi

"Goketsu-bushii" ("The Heroes' Song"), Kumamoto

> *NnMY* Side 18, Item #158
> Voice: Akasaka Ko-ume
>
> *King* LP SKM 37 Side 2, Item #1
> Voice: Kikutarō
>
> *King* LP SKM 37 Side 1, Item #4
> Voice: Yoshizawa Hiroshi

"Tairyō utai-komi-uta" ("Fine Fishing Medley"), Miyagi

> national version
> ("Saitara-bushi" and "Toshima jinku" only):
> *NnMY* Side 4, Item #31
> Voice: Azuma Momoya
>
> *NHK* No. 4, Item #2
> Voice: Azuma Momoya
>
> local version (above songs sometimes preceded by a third song, such as "Doya-bushi" or "Kesen-numa jinku"):
> *NHK–R* "Tohoku" ('The Northeast) I–3–*A*
> Voice: Akama Masao (Rinsui) singing "Doya-bushi"
> Voice: Azuma Momoya singing "Saitara-bushi" and "Toshima jinku"

"Takayama ondo" ("*Ondo* from Takayama"), Gifu

> *Victor* LP MC–241
> Voice: Satō Yoshio

"Tanuki odori" ("Raccoon Dance"), Kagawa

> *Toshiba* 45 rpm TP–1491
> Voice: Hamada Kiichi (II)

"*Tanto*-bushi" ("The *Tanto* Song"), Akita

> *NnMY* Side 5, Item #45
> Voice: Kurosawa Sōichi/Miichi
>
> *TMDZS* Side 8, Item #1
> Voice: Hasegawa Hisako

"Teradomari okesa," Niigata

    NHK No. 6, Item #8
        Voice: Tsukiko/Gesshi

"Tsugaru *aiya*-bushi" (*"Aiya!* Song from Tsugaru"), Aomori

    NnMY Side 2, Item #13
        Voice: Uno Kiyomi

    MGRK Side 3–B, Item #(b)13
        Voice: Sudō Eiko

    King LP LKF 1040 Side 1, Item #3
        Voice: Kasai Chieko

"Tsugaru-bayashi" ("The Tsugaru Band"), Aomori

    Victor 45 rpm MV–544–S
        Voice: Asari Miki

    TMDZS Side 2, Item #7
        Voice: Sudō Un'ei

"Tsugaru *jongara*-bushi" ("The Breakdown Song from Tsugaru"), Aomori

    TMDZS Side 2, Item #3
        Voice: Kimura Yogorō

    Victor 45 rpm MV–551–S
        Voice: Asari Miki

    NnMY Side 1, Item #7
        Voice: Satō Ritsu

"Tsugaru owara-bushi"; "Tsugaru ohara-bushi" ("The *Owara* Song from Tsugaru"), Aomori

    NHK No. 2, Item #5
        Voice: Ichinohe Mitsuharu

    NnMY Side 1, Item #9
        Words: Nomiya Shin'ichi
        Voice: Suzuki Taki

    TMDZS Side 1, Item #2
        Voice: Yamanouchi Tatsu

    Victor LP MU–78–S
        Voice: Asari Miki

"Tsugaru tanto-bushi" ("The *Tanto* Song from Tsugaru"), Aomori
   TMDZS Side 4, Item #3
      Voice: Ono Ichiko

"Tsugaru yama-uta" ("Song from Tsugaru for Work in the Mountains"), Aomori
   Columbia 45 rpm SAS-6141
      Voice: Fujiwara Yoshinori
   Columbia LP DLS-4039
      Voice: Asari Miki
   TMDZS Side 1, Item #3
      Voice: Wakamiya Gorō

"Tsurusaki odori" ("Dance from Tsurusaki"), Ōita
   NnMY Side 19, Item #162
      Voices (members of the Tsurusaki Odori Conservation Society):
         Araki Ken
         Oka Ritsuko
   NHK No. 9, Item #11
      Voice: Ikemi Rintarō
   King LP SS-5045
      Voice: Kobana (geisha)

"Tsukudajima bon-odori-uta" ("Bon-Dance Song from Tsukudajima"), Tōkyō
   NnMY Side 8, Item #75
      Voice: Izeki Tatsunosuke

"Ume no uta-genka" ("A Song-Quarrel from Ume"), Ōita
   King 45 rpm BS-5262
      Voices (alternating):
         Oita Tamachiyo
         Ono Mari

"Yagi-bushi" ("Song from Yagi"), Gumma, Tochigi
   Victor LP MC-75-S ("Kunisada Chūji" story)
   Victor LP MC-76-S ("Suzuki Mondo" story)
      Voice on both recordings: Horigome Genta IV

"Yasaburō bushii" ("The Yasaburō Song"), Aomori
 Victor 45 rpm MV–567–S
 Voice: Asari Miki

"Yasugi-bushi" ("Song from Yasugi"), Shimane
 King LP KR 15 Side 1, Item #6
 Voice: Kuroda Yukiko

"Yosare"
Aomori: Tsugaru Region
 NHK No. 2, Item #2
 Voice: Takahashi Tsuya

Aomori: Shimokita Peninsula
 Toshiba 45 rpm TP–1719
 Voice: Natsuzaka Kikuo

"Zarantoshō" (also known as "Zarantoshō-bushi
and "Ine-age-uta"), Miyagi
 TMDZS Side 17, Item #3
 Voice: Sasaki Hiroshi/ō

"Zeni-fuki-uta" ("Minting Song"), Miyagi
 King 45 rpm BS–5252
 Voice: Harada Naoyuki

Bibliography

> The chief glory of every people arises from its authors ... I shall not think my employment useless or ignoble, if by my assistance foreign nations, and distant ages, gain access to the propagators of knowledge, and understand the teachers of truth ...
>
> Samuel Johnson, in his
> Preface to his *Dictionary* (1755)

This bibliography is a practical sampler of Japanese folk-song collections and pertinent reference works on Japanese history, society, and culture, but is by no means exhaustive.

Asano Kenji. *Chūsei kayō.* (Songs of the Middle Ages.) Tokyo: Hanawa Shobō, Shōwa 39 (1964).

> A history of folk and popular songs from Japan's Middle Ages, the twelfth century to the Tokugawa Period.

Asano Kenji. *Nihon no min'yō.* (The folk songs of Japan.) Tokyo: Iwanami Shinsho, 1966.

> A cultural history of Japanese folk song.

Berger, Donald Paul, ed. *Folk Songs of Japan.* New York: Oak Publications, 1972.

A useful book for Western singers, musicians, and composers. The choice of fifty-four songs is excellent. As of 1980, it is the only such collection in which entire Japanese song texts are given in romanization, that is, written in English letters. Both the romanizations and the English translations could use some revision, but Berger's melodic transcriptions are accurate, and his arrangements are both practical and subtle—among the best in any Western collection of Japanese folk songs. For guitar, flute, and unspecified percussion. He also includes some of Machida Kashō's superb transcriptions.

Borton, Hugh. *Peasant Uprisings in Japan of the Tokugawa Period*. Second edition, with a new introduction. New York: Paragon Book Reprint Corp., 1968.

Bownas, Geoffrey. *Japanese Rainmaking and Other Folk Practices*. London: George Allen & Unwin Ltd., 1963.

Most of the author's examples are from the Kinki region on Honshu and Kyushu. Bownas describes Bon, the New Year, "Births, Marriages, and Deaths," taboos, village life.

Boxer, C. R. *Jan Compagnie in Japan, 1600–1817. Essay on the Cultural, Artistic and Scientific Influences Exercised by the Hollanders in Japan from the Seventeenth to the Nineteenth Centuries*. Authorized reprint (with corrections) of second revised edition (1950). London: Oxford University Press, 1968.

De Becker, J. E. *Yoshiwara, the Nightless City*. Reprint of third edition (1905). New York: Frederick Publications, 1960.

As part of his study, the author discusses some contemporary geisha slang, bordello and entertainment district literature, art, songs, and dances.

Embree, John F. *Japanese Peasant Songs*. Philadelphia: American Folklore Society, 1944.

A study of several folk songs, such as "Kuma rokuchōshi" from Kumamoto, where the author lived for a while. He based his study on songtexts he and his two assistants compiled and annotated. He writes extensively on how, where, and by whom each song was performed. The only thing missing in this careful study is a musical score, but Embree's ear for music still shows in his descriptions.

Erskine, William Hugh. *Japanese Festival and Calendar Lore.* Tokyo: Kyo Bun Kwan, 1933.

Fujimoto Shūjō. *Min' yō senshū: shamisen bunka-fu.* (A selection of folk songs: notations of the shamisen culture.) Tokyo: Hōgakusha, Shōwa 44 (1969).

This seven-volume series gives the outlines of shamisen accompaniments for over fifty folk songs. They are transcribed in a modern shamisen notation on a three-line staff, a line to a shamisen string. Mnemonics are included. The vocal melodies are outlined under the staves in another modern form of notation using Arabic numerals, which is also very popular with the Chinese.

Fujiwara Yoichi. *A Dialect Grammar of Japanese.* Monumenta Nipponica monograph, Number 20. Tokyo: Sophia University Press, 1965.

Fujiwara Yoichi. *Nihongo hōgen bumpō no kenkyū.* (Studies in the grammar of Japanese dialects.) Tokyo: Iwanami Shoten, 1949.

Fukagata Hisashi. *Nagasaki no min'yō.* (Folk songs of Nagasaki.) Tokyo: Kenkōsha, Shōwa 44 (1969).

Geinōsha Kenkyūkai, eds. *Nihon shomin bunka shiryō shūsei.* (A compilation of historical materials and records of Japanese popular culture.) Tokyo: San-ichi Shobō.

As of 1973 nine volumes had been published of a projected fifteen. The materials include popular visual arts; games; and urban, local, and rural folk songs and dances, among them children's songs. Magnificent reproductions of contemporary illustrative drawings and other documentation.

Hattori Ryūtarō, ed. *Japanese Folk Songs with Piano Accompaniment*. Piano accompaniment arranged by Teiji Miyahara and Masao Shinohara. Verse translated into English by Iwao Matsuhara. Explanatory notes by Ryutaro Hattori. Tokyo: The Japan Times, 1971 (seventh edition).

Both this book and the author's *Traditional Folk Songs of Japan* (Tokyo: Ongaku-mo-tomo-sha, 1966) are pioneer collections of Japanese folk songs for Westerners and Western-oriented Japanese. In both books, after the first verse or two of a song, the texts are not given in romanization.

Hattori Ryūtarō. *Nihon min'yō no hakken*. (Discovery of Japanese folk song.) Tokyo: Hironsha, 1958.

The author's emphasis is on the rural and local backgrounds of the songs, their surroundings and their moods.

Hattori Ryūtarō. *Nihon min'yō zenshū*. (A complete collection of Japanese folk songs.) Tokyo: Kadokawa Shoten, Shōwa 40 (1965).

This book of 320 songs has skeletal melodies for many songs and includes their most popular lyrics. It has background commentary on each song and good regional maps. It is invaluable as a small, handy reference for many well-known folk songs and for quite a few that are less well known.

Hattori Tomoji. *Nihon min'yō-ron*. (On Japanese folk songs.) Tokyo: Shindokushosha, 1965.

The author discusses modern folk song. He makes comparisons of individual folk songs and folk-song styles, for example of the "Rural 'Song on Three Levels'" as sung by a geisha from Kashiwazaki City (Niigata) and as sung by Ko-uta Katsutarō. He also makes melodic comparisons with some Korean and European folk songs. He writes about folk instruments and about traditional children's songs, the *warabe-uta,* and their connection with folk songs. This book and the author's *Nihon no min'yō*

(The folk songs of Japan) (Tokyo: Sani-ichi Shobō, 1959) contain important background information on many folk songs, such as "A Song on Three Levels."

Heibonsha, eds. *Nihon minzoku taikei*. (An outline of Japanese folk customs.) Tokyo: Heibonsha, Shōwa 37 (1962). Thirteen volumes.

Hepburn, J. C. *A Japanese-English and English-Japanese Dictionary*. Fourth edition. Tokyo: Z. P. Maruya & Co., Ltd., 1888.

The author cites many popular song types and musical expressions current in the 1870s and 1880s in Japan, including idioms, proverbs, and poetic phrases.

Hirota Ryūtarō and Fujii Kiyomi. *Nihon min'yō-shū*. (Anthology of Japanese folk songs.) Tokyo: Shunjusha, 1930.)

Hori Ichirō. *Waga kuni minkan shinkō-shi no kenkyū*. (Studies in the history of our country's folk beliefs.) Osaka: Sōgensha, 1953).

Joly, Henry L. *Legend in Japanese Art: A description of historical episodes, legendary characters, folk-lore, myths, religious symbolism. Illustrated in the arts of old Japan.* London: J. Lane, 1908.

This book has been reissued by the Charles E. Tuttle Company (Rutland, 1967). *Legend in Japanese Art* and the writings of Lafcadio Hearn have been an introduction to Japanese folklore for at least three generations of Westerners, mine among them.

Kadokawa Teiji, Naramoto Tatsuya, et al, eds. *Zusetsu Nihon shomin seikatsu-shi*. (Illustrated history of Japan's social life and customs.) Tokyo: Kawade Shobō Shinsha, 1961.

These eight volumes survey the social history of Japan from earliest times to the present.

Kaneda Kuzan. *Kyōdo geijutsu: Nihon min'yō.* (Regional, local, rural arts: Japanese folk songs). Tokyo: Kōbunsha, Shōwa 6 (1931).

Fifty-eight songs.

Katō Hidetoshi, ed. and trans. *Japanese Popular Culture: Studies in Mass Communication and Cultural Change.* Rutland: Charles E. Tuttle Company, 1959.

These essays deal with topics related to folk song, such as postwar Japanese popular songs and the "Yagi-bushi" hero Kunisada Chūji in desperado *(yakuza)* fiction, language as communication in Japan, popular fiction, and the movies.

Kawade Shobō Shinsha, eds. *Nihon rekishi daijiten* (Encyclopedia of Japanese history.) Tokyo: Kawade Shobō Shinsha, Shōwa 31–35 (1956–1960).

This encyclopedia is in twenty volumes. There are two additional volumes: *Nihon rekishi chizu* (Historical atlas of Japan) and *Nihon rekishi nenpyō* (Chronological tables of Japanese history).

Keene, Donald. *The Japanese Discovery of Europe: 1720–1830.* Stanford: Stanford University Press, 1969.

This is the revised edition of *The Japanese Discovery of Europe: Honda Toshiaki and Other Discoveries* 1720–1798 (London: Rutledge and Kegan Paul Ltd.). Also see the author's *Battles of Coxinga* (London: Taylor's Foreign Press, 1951).

Keene, Donald. *World Within Walls. Japanese Literature of the Pre-Modern Era 1600–1867.* New York: Holt, Rhinehart and Winston, 1976.

Kindaichi Kyōsuke and Kindaichi Haruhiko, eds. *Meikai kogo jiten.* (A precise dictionary of archaic words.) Tokyo: Sandeidō, Shōwa 38 (1963).

Kodera Yukichi, ed. *Kyōdo min'yō buyō jiten.* (Dictionary of regional folk song and dance.) Revised and enlarged edition. Tokyo: Fuzambō, 1941.

Koizumi Fumio, ed. *Warabe-uta no kenkyū.* (A Study of warabe-uta.) Title in English: *Game Songs of Japanese Children: Report of a Group-Study on Warabeuta of Tokyo in 1961.* Tokyo: Warabe-uta no Kenkyū Kenkō, 1969.

Among its many beauties, this two-volume work contains excellent English translations of the traditional children's songs it includes. The comparative scores are a musician's delight. The work includes a study of these songs' relationship and connections with other song genres, and movement-by-movement drawings or photographs of the games. Both the children and the scholars appear to have had a wonderful time putting the book together.

Kubo Kenwo. *Minami Nippon min'yō kyoku-shū.* (Anthology of folk-song melodies of southern Japan.) Tokyo: Ongaku-no-tomo-sha, 1960.

This book contains detailed melodies in Western notation of many major folk songs of southern Japan, including the Amami-Ōshima islands. It also has the song texts, though these are not always accompanied by local readings of the words. There are, however, notes on local dialects.

Kubo Kenwo. *Minami Nihon warabe-uta fudoki.* (A topography of children's songs of southern Japan.) Tokyo: Ongaku-no-tomo-sha, 1964.

This anthology gives both words and melodies, and includes children's songs from Okinawa.

Machida Hitoshi. *Shinano no min'yō.* (Folk songs of Shinano Province.) Tokyo: Ongaku-no-tomo-sha, 1965.

Detailed melodies and the texts of two hundred songs from Nagano Prefecture.

Machida Kashō. *Nihon min'yō shikashū.* (A beautiful poetic anthology of Japanese folk songs.) Tokyo: Mirai-sha, 1954.

A penetrating, affectionate look at the spectrum of Japanese folk song. Machida includes many comparative song texts and scores both of individual songs, such as the "Northern Kyushu Coal-Miner's Song" from Fukuoka, and of forms of song, such as the *okesa*.

Machida Kashō and Asano Kenji. *Nihon min'yō-shū.* (Anthology of Japanese folk songs.) Tokyo: Iwanami Shoten, Shōwa 40 (1965).

This is one of the finest of the pocketsize folk-song collections with its many footnotes on the history of each song in the book, its notes on dialect expressions, its mention of the shamisen tuning and basic verse pattern for each song, its choice of texts—many verses included are not widely known but are of the utmost literary and historical importance—and its excellent bibliography. Here the authors' emphasis is on text rather than on music: few melodies are given.

Machida Kashō and Asano Kenji. *Warabe-uta: Nihon no denshō dōyō.* (*Warabe-uta:* the traditional children's song of Japan.) Tokyo: Iwanami Shoten, Shōwa 43 (1968).

This anthology contains both music and annotated song texts. There is a large-scale bibliography that is of great value not only to musicians and writers, but to historians.

Matisoff, Susan. *The Legend of Semimaru, Blind Musician of Japan.* New York: Columbia University Press, 1978.

Matsumoto Shinhachirō. *Min'yō no rekishi.* (History of folk song.) Tokyo: Sekkasha, 1965.

Matsunaga Goichi. *Nihon no komori-uta: minzokugaku-teki apurōchi.* (The Japanese lullaby: an anthropological approach.) Tokyo: Kiinokuniya Shinsho, 1954.

Migita, C. I. (Migita Isao), ed. Title in English: *The 1st Folk Song Book of Nippon.* Title in Japanese: *Eigo de utau*

Nihon min'yō. (Japanese folk songs to sing in English.) Tokyo: Kawai Gakufu, 1970.

This book contains the outline melodies for thirty-six songs. Although the English texts are in forced-rhyme verse and only the first one or two stanzas of each song are romanized, it is full of useful notes on each song. The chronological table in the back includes titles of Japanese folk-song collections dating back over four hundred years, that also contain names of folksingers, poets, and composers.

Mikado Tempu, ed. *Nihon min'yō zenshū.* (A complete anthology of Japanese folk songs.) Tokyo: Shimfonii (Symphony) Gakufu Shuppansha, Volume 1, 1970; Volume 2, 1973.

This collection gives the vocal lines, shakuhachi intros, and shamisen tunings. In effect, it is a collection of lead sheets for four hundred songs, most of which are available on commercial recordings.

Minzokugaku Kenkyūjo, eds. *Sōgō Nihon minzoku goi.* (Comprehensive vocabulary of Japanese folkways.) Tokyo: Heibonsha, 1955–56.

Illustrations and quotations are included in this five-volume work. There are also about 35,000 folk terms not found in ordinary dictionaries. This vocabulary incorporates much of the material in *Bunrui nōson goi* (Classified vocabulary of farming villages), an earlier reference work by the folklorist Yanagida Kunio (published in Tokyo, 1947–48).

Miyoshi Ikko, ed. *Edo-go jiten.* (A dictionary of Edo-Period language.) Tokyo: Sei-a-bō, Shōwa 46 (1971).

Morris, Ivan. *The Nobility of Failure.* New York: New American Library, 1976.

The author's valedictory, this work is a sympathetic study of the defeated and beloved heroes of Japanese history from ancient times to the present. As a major part of his study, Morris discusses portrayals of these heroes in folk and popular arts, including music.

Nagano Prefecture Institute of Music Education (Nagano-ken ongaku kyōiku gakkai). *Shinano no warabe-uta.* (Traditional children's songs of Shinano Province.) Tokyo: Ongaku-no-tomo-sha, 1965.

Texts and melodies of children's songs from Nagano Prefecture.

Nakai Kōjirō, Maruyama Shinobu, and Misumi Haruo. *Nihon min'yō jiten.* (A dictionary of Japanese folk song.) Tokyo: Tōkyōdō, Shōwa 47 (1972).

This dictionary includes information on commercial recordings and on many folksingers.

Nakauchi Chōji and Tamura Nishio, eds. *Zokkyoku zenshū/ zokuyō zenshū.* (Complete collection of folk and popular songs.) Volume 7 of *Nihon ongyoku zenshū* (A complete collection of Japanese songs accompanied by shamisen). Tokyo: Risōsha, Shōwa 2 (1927).

A collection of texts of 271 folk and popular songs.

Nakayama Yasumasa, ed. *Nankun jiten.* (A dictionary of difficult readings of characters.) Fourteenth edition. Tokyo: Tōkyōdō, Shōwa 42 (1967).

Among other good dictionaries of unusual and hard-to-read names, surnames, geographical names, and terms are A. P. Abolmasov's *Slovar' yaponskikh geograficheskikh nazvanii* (Dictionary of Japanese geographical names, Moscow, 1959), Araki Ryōzō's *Nanori jiten* (Dictionary of personal names, Tokyo, 1959). NHK's *Nandoku seishi* (Hard-to-read surnames, Tokyo, 1964), and P. G. O'Neill's *Japanese Names* (New York, 1972).

Nippon Hōsō Kyōkai, eds. *Nihon min'yō taikan.* (Panorama of Japanese folk song.) Tokyo: NHK, 1942–1969.

This nine-volume work contains thousands of folk songs—often over ten versions of one song—in detailed Western notation that frequently includes instrumental accompaniment; songtexts and extensive background information; some illustrations; and names of folksingers. It is proof that every place in Japan is rich in beautiful folk songs, despite modest disclaimers.

Nobarasha, eds. *Nihon no min'yō.* (Folk songs of Japan.) Revised edition. Tokyo: Nobarasha, Sōwa 43 (1968).

Contains words and detailed melodies for 239 folk songs, transcribed both in Western and modern Sino-Japanese numerical notation. Many of the melodies were transcribed by Machida Kashō and Hattori Ryūtarō. The book includes some "new-style folk songs" by Nakayama Shimpei and others.

Philippi, Donald L., translator. *Kojiki.* Tokyo: University of Tokyo Press, 1968.

Philippi, Donald L., translator. *This Wine of Peace, This Wine of Laughter: A complete anthology of Japan's earliest songs.* New York: Grossman Publishers, 1968, with Tokyo: Mushinsha.

Roggendorf, Joseph, ed. *Studies in Japanese Culture: Tradition and Experiment.* Tokyo: Sophia University, 1965.

Sakamoto Tarō, ed. *Fūzoku jiten.* (Dictionary of social customs.) Tokyo: Tōkyōdō, 1963.

A useful general reference work on customs up to and including the Meiji Era (1868–1912).

Sakane Iwawo, Fukuoka Hiroshi, and Hirata Etsurō, eds. *Saga no warabe-uta.* (Traditional children's songs of Saga Prefecture.) Tokyo Ongaku-no-tomo-sha, 1960.

Sansom, George. *An Historical Grammar of Japanese.* Oxford: The Clarendon Press, 1966.

Shimonaka Kunihiko, ed. *Ongaku jiten.* (Encyclopedia of music.) Tokyo: Heibonsha, 1966-67. Five volumes.

Shimonaka Yasaburō, ed. *Heibonsha Dai-jiten.* Tokyo: Heibonsha, Shōwa 28-29 (1953-54).

A thirteen-volume encyclopedia that includes many slang and dialect entries.

Sonoyama Min'pei. *Hyūga min'yō.* Title in English: *101 Folk-Songs of Hiuga.* Tokyo: Ongaku-no-tomo-sha, Shōwa 32 (1957).

Folk songs of Miyazaki Prefecture. The author makes important points about the songs through his transcriptions of the melodies. For example, he puts a key signature in parentheses to show that one may sing the melody in either of two modes. Songtexts and some background information are included.

Suzuki Tōjō. *Gijinmei jiten.* (Dictionary of made-up names.) Tokyo: Tōkyōdō, 1963.

This dictionary contains about two thousand slang terms created from made-up personal names, for example, "Gennai" (seafood), "Manukeda Koreya" (you're a jackass), "Nukesaku" (Simpleton), "Ebicha Shikibu" (a girl student).

Suzuki Tōzō and Hirota Eitarō. *Koji kotowaza jiten.* (Dictionary of historical allusions and proverbs.) Tokyo: Tōkyōdō, 1956. A second volume published in 1961.

Takeda Chūichirō, ed. *Tōhoku min'yō-shū.* (Anthology of folk songs of the Northeast.) Tokyo: NHK, 1956-1966.

Six volumes, one to a prefecture. Includes the song texts and detailed Western notation for the folk songs, often for their instrumental accompaniments and related pieces of music. Background notes.

Takeuchi Tsutomu. *Uta no furusato: Nihon no min'yō o tazunete.* (The Back Home of song: seeing about Japanese folk song.) Tokyo: Ongaku-no-tomo-sha, Shōwa 44 (1969).

A history of many folk songs and folk-song forms.

Tanabe Hisao. *Nihon no gakki: Nihon gakki jiten.* (Musical instruments of Japan: a dictionary of Japanese musical instruments.) Tokyo: Sōshisha, Shōwa 39 (1964).

Tōjō Misao, ed. *Zengoku hogen jiten.* (A dictionary of dialects nationwide.) Twenty-sixth edition. Tokyo: Tōkyōdō, Shōwa 42 (1967).

This is a basic reference for the many Japanese dialects. A supplement was published in 1954 by the same company: *Hyōjūngobiki bunrui hōgen jiten* (A classified dictionary of dialect words listed by standard words).

Tsurumi, Kazuko. *Social Change and the Individual: Japan Before and After Defeat in World War II.* Princeton: Princeton University Press, 1970.

Ueda, Makoto. *Literary and Art Theories in Japan.* Cleveland: The Press of Western Reserve University, 1967.

Umegaki Minoru. *Ingo jiten.* (Dictionary of secret languages.) Tokyo: Tōkyōdō, 1956.

From the Nara Period (645–794) to the present. Includes professional argots, thieves' cant, women's expressions, and students' slang.

Vogel, Ezra F. *Japan's New Middle Class: The Salary Man and His Family in a Tokyo Suburb.* Berkeley: University of California Press, 1965.

Yamanaka Jōta. *Hōgen zokugo gogen jiten.* (An etymological dictionary of dialects, slang, and colloquialisms.) Tokyo: Azekura shobō, 1970.

Yanagida Kunio. *Min'yō oboegaki.* (Notes on folk songs.) Tokyo: Sogensha, 1941.

Among the vast number of words by this superb folklorist are *Ritō seikatsu no kenkyū* (Studies of life on the outlying islands, Tokyo, 1966), studies of customs on smaller islands within the radius of prefectures on Honshu, Shikoku, and Kyushu; *Minzokugaku jiten* (An encyclopedia of folklore, Tokyo, 1951); and *Yukiguni no minzoku* (Folk customs of the Snow Country) (Tokyo, 1944, with Miki Shigeru).

Yazaki, Takeo. *Social Change and the City in Japan: From Earliest Times Through the Industrial Revolution.* Translated by David L. Swain. Tokyo: Sophia University Press, 1968.

Index

"Aiya! Song," 63; from
   Amori, 9
"Akita Ondo," 37–38, 78
Animism, 6–7
Annals of Japan (Nihon Shoki), 3
"Autumn Song for Work in the
   Mountains," 34
Baka-bayashi, 67
"Ballad from Aikawa," 23, 27,
   57, 68; (Sado Island in
   Niigata), 47, 65, 81
"Ballad from Ōmi," 21, 67
*Ballads-and-Airs Scene (Ko-uta
   no chimata)*, 19
Banquet-and party songs, 37,
   40–42, 44, 50, 54
"Barley-and-Such Song,"
   12–13, 31, 34, 65
Bazan the Woodchopper, 19
"Beach Song," 43; from Ibaraki,
   38, 64
Blessing Words, 7
"Bon Song from Sōma," 8, 48.
   See also O-Bon
Book of Songs (Shr jing), 20

Bon Festival. *See* O-Bon
"Breakdown Song from
   Tsugaru," 9, 64
Buddhism, 6–7. *See also* O-Bon

Children's songs, 2, 62–63
*Collection of a Myriad Leaves
   (Man' yōshū)*, 3, 20
Communal songs, 8–9, 42
Congratulation songs, 7–8,
   50, 62
Counting songs, 62–63

"Dance from Awa," 8–9,
   68, 81
Dodoitsu, 43–44, 81

Enka, 44–45, 86
"Esashi oiwake," 55–57,
   64–66, 68, 79, 82;
   musical example, 58

"Factory-girls' Song," 84,
   musical example, 85
Festival for Souls. *See* O-Bon
Festival of Lanterns. *See* O-Bon

[123]

Index

"Fine Fishing Medley," 65; from Miijagi, 68; from Haragama, 69; musical example, 70
Folk song (min' yō): def. of, 1–2; as political gauge, 26; hist. background of, 2–8, 10–11, 13–14, 16–22, 24–26, 34, 40, 43–44, 47, 54, 56, 62, 78, 87–88. *See also* Song forms and themes; Shin min yō

Geisha, 40–41, 43–44, 50, 78, 80; famous singers, 21, 23–24
"Grain-pounding Song from Awa," 33
Guilds, 4, 21

Haiku, 10, 28
Ha-uta, 21, 43–44, 83
Hayashi, 5, 67, 74, 77
Hayashi-kotoba, 42, 74–78; musical example, 75–77
Heian Period, 7, 26, 57
Horiuchi-school, 22–23

Jinku, 47–48
"Jinku from Toshima," 64, 72

Kakegoe, 5, 67–74, 77–78; musical example, 73
"Kanchororin Song," 7, 64
Kanginshū (Anthology of Leisure Recitations), 16
Kitahara, Hakushū, 3, 26
Kodera, Gyokuchō, 19
Kojiki. See *Record of Ancient Matters*

Ko-uta, 16, 23, 43, 81
Kudoki, 57

"Late Autumn Rain," 8. *See also* "New 'Late Autumn Rain' "
Love songs (every mood), 31–38, 41–42, 49, 56–57
Lullaby, 13, 41, 67
Lyrics: importance of, 25; linguistic variations in, 27–38; parody in, 33–34; poetry in, 2–3, 7, 12, 19–20, 25–28, 32, 44, 46–47, 54–57, 63–65, 77–78, 87; titles of, 38–39, 64

Machida, Kashō, 1, 19–20, 24
Masao, Suzuki, 72–74
"Matsuyama Dance," 29
Meiji Era, 87
Melodious recitation. See Rōei
Min' yō. *See* folk song
Muneyasu Anthology of Airs (Muneyasu ko-uta-shu), 17–18
Muromachi Period, 16, 19, 43
Musical instruments: fue (woodwind), 44, 67, 82, 86; kokyū (viol), 45, 81–82, 86; koto (zither), 44, 55, 81–82; biwa (lute), 25, 67; percussion, 48, 54, 66–67, 74, 82–83, 87; shakuhachi (woodwind), 45, 54–55, 66, 86, 88; shamisen, 17, 42–44, 54–55, 66–68, 78, 81–82, 86, 88; basic shamisen

Index

tuning, 80, 86; shamisen tuning example, 80; Tsugaru shamisen, 21, 79; sanshin, 79–80, 82; taiko, 86; soprano recorder, 86

Nara Period, 3, 7
"New 'Bon Festival Song from Hokkaidō,'" 65. *See also* O-Bon
"New 'Late Autumn Rain,'" 19–20, 24. *See also* "Late Autumn Rain"
"New 'Song of Sōma,'" 24, 73–74; musical example, 72. *See also* "Song of Sōma"
Nom d'artiste, 22–24
Norito. *See* Blessing Words
"Nursemaid's Song from Itsuki Village," 41, 64

Obako, 57
O-Bon, 6, 8, 39, 45–48, 65, 87; dance songs 47–48. *See also* "Bon Song from Soma"
Oiwake, 54–55
Okesa, 24, 47
Ondo, 57
Otsu-e, 62
Owara, 47–48
"Owara Song from Etchu," 9, 82

"Packhorseman's Art Song from Esashi," 12, 31, 44, 55
"Packhorseman's Song from Komoro," 7, 29, 36–38. *See also* "Sōma Packhorseman's Song"
Packhorseman's songs, 36, 54–57
Patriotic songs, 56–57
Performing techniques, 1, 3–5, 10, 14, 17, 24–26, 40–45, 47, 54–55, 57, 65–69, 77–81, 86–87
Place-of-origin songs, 13–14

Record of Ancient Matters (Kojiki), 3, 5–7, 78
"Refrain from Soma," 9–10, 64
Rōei, 25
Rythmn patterns, 5, 37–38, 68–70, 73–74, 77–78, 84–85; musical example, 75–78
Ryutatsu's Anthology of Airs (Ryutatsu ko-uta-shū), 18

Saimon, 67
"Saitara's Song," 24, 37, 64, 69; musical example, 70
Samurai, 18–19, 28, 79
"Shimoda Song," 14, 35, 65–66, 81
"Shinano Oiwake," 37
Shinjū, 18–19
Shin min 'yō, 87
Shintō, 3, 5–7, 16
Shōwa Era, 87
Singlemindedness: concept of, 21–22; cult of, 20
"Sōma Barley-hulling Song," 37, 64; musical example, 72
"Sōma Packhorseman's Song," 11

Song forms and themes, 2–3, 7–14, 16, 21–22, 24–26, 40–65, 68–78, 84–85
"Song from Tsugaru for Work in the Mountains," 35
"Song from Yagi," 47, 64
"Song from Yasugi," 11, 79
Song keys, 84
"Song of Kiso," 11
"Song of Sōma," 11. See also "New 'Song of Sōma;'" "Refrain from Sōma"
"Song on Three Levels," 39, 41–42, 65, 81
Songs about songs, 8–9
Spoken song. See Hayashi; Hayashi-kotoba; Rōei
Suiko Period, 3

Taishō Era, 87
Takeda, Chūichirō 19–20, 24
Take-mono, 88
"Tanto Song," 62
"Tanto Song from Tsugaru," 74; musical example, 76

Ta-ue-zōshi (Copybook of Rice Planting), 16
Teachers of folk songs, 4, 21–22
"Tea-Cutters' Song," 3, 20
Tokugawa Period, 11, 16, 18–22, 26, 44, 47, 54
Topography of Children's Songs from Southern Japan (Minami Nihon warabe-uta fudoki), 26
Traveling verses, 11–13
"Tree-pruning Song," 36
Trousseau-carrying Songs, 48–49
"Tsugaru Aiya! Song," 64, 66

Warabe-uta, 2, 62–63
Western influence, 2, 21, 48–49, 84, 86–88
Woodchopping Folk Songs (Shōso fūzoku uta), 19
Work songs, 7, 50–57; musical example, 85

Yoshare songs, 63